Math 4 Today

Grade 5

by Donna Pearson

Frank Schaffer Publications®

Author: Donna Pearson
Editor: Sara Bierling
Interior Designer: Lori Kibbey

Frank Schaffer Publications®

Send all inquiries to:
Frank Schaffer Publications
8720 Orion Place
Columbus, Ohio 43240-2111

Math 4 Today—grade 5

ISBN: 0-7682-3205-8

7 8 9 10 PAT 12 11 10 09

Math 4 Today

Table of Contents

Introduction

What is Math 4 Today?

Math 4 Today is a comprehensive yet quick and easy-to-use supplement sequenced to complement any fifth-grade math curriculum. Twenty-four essential math skills and concepts are reviewed in only ten minutes each day during a four-day period (presumably Monday through Thursday) with a 20-minute evaluation each fifth day (Friday).

How Does It Work?

Unlike many math programs, *Math 4 Today* is designed on a continuous spiral so that concepts are repeated weekly. This book supplies four problems a day for four days, covering a 40-week period based on the curriculum for fifth grade. A separate ten-problem test is provided for the fifth day of each week.

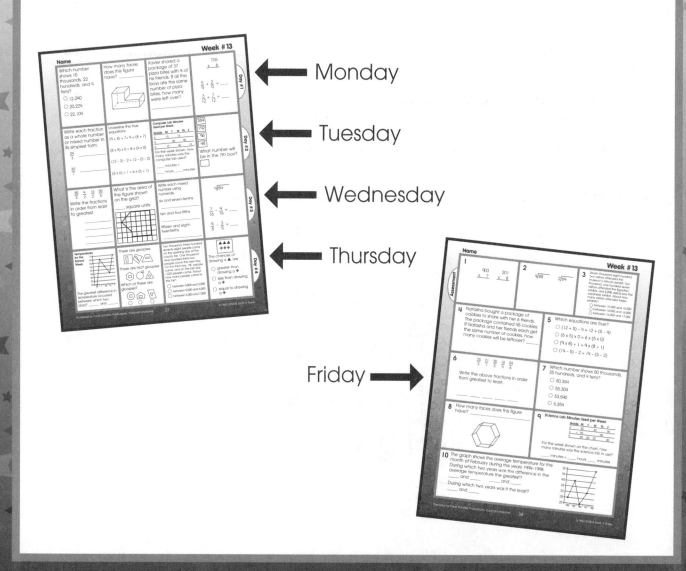

Monday

Tuesday

Wednesday

Thursday

Friday

Introduction (cont.)

Answer keys are provided for both daily drills and assessments (see pages 93–112). Although the concepts and skills are individually categorized, most are interrelated so that many opportunities for practice and evaluation exist. A skills and concepts chart (including objectives) and a scope and sequence chart are provided.

How Was It Developed?

Math 4 Today was created in response to a need for ongoing practice after a skill had been addressed in the basal text. With the usual methods, a skill would be covered and then almost abandoned until it reappeared (sometimes) in a six-week cumulative review. With the growing emphasis on standardized testing, the necessity for experience with test styles and semantics also becomes apparent. We began with four daily problems written on the board for students to complete while attendance was being taken. After completion, the class would briefly check and discuss the work. The problems and methods we used evolved and expanded over the years. Now, I duplicate the weekly pages for students and use overhead transparencies to check and discuss.

What Are the Benefits?

The daily approach of *Math 4 Today* provides risk-taking challenges, higher-level thinking exercises, problem-solving strategies, and necessary drills, emphasizing areas that frequently give students difficulty, such as subtraction with regrouping and word problems. The pages target test-taking skills by incorporating the style and syntax of standardized tests such as the TAKS (Texas Assessment of Knowledge and Skills). Because of its consistent format, *Math 4 Today* not only offers opportunities for instruction but also serves as an excellent diagnostic tool.

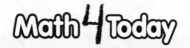

Assessment

In addition to formal assessments, ongoing informal assessment should be part of everyday instruction. This includes listening to students' responses to questions and observing students at work.

At the beginning of the school year, do a baseline assessment of each student. To do this, watch students in a variety of situations, such as at lunch, on the playground, in line, in group activities, and during individual work. An early assessment should include factors such as social (communication and cooperation), behavioral (confidence and self-control), and academic (organization and work habits) skills.

Throughout the year, you can use a variety of assessment strategies.

- questioning
- observation
- textbook tests
- teacher-developed tests
- rubrics
- student self-evaluation
- journal review
- portfolio review
- checklists
- conferences

Also, use the following assessment rubric when examining students' work. Have students become familiar with this rubric so that they can do self-assessment.

3 The student's performance or work sample shows a thorough understanding of the topic. Work is clearly explained with examples and/or words, all calculations are correct , and explanations reflect reasoning beyond the simplicity of the calculations.

2 The student's performance or work sample shows a good understanding of the topic. There may be some errors in calculations, but the work reflects a general knowledge of details and a reasonable understanding of mathematical ideas.

1 The student's performance or work sample shows a limited understanding of the topic. The written work does not reflect understanding of mathematical ideas, and examples contain errors.

0 The student's performance or work sample is too weak to evaluate, or nonexistent.

Test-Taking Tips

1. Read through the entire problem before starting to solve it.

2. Use scrap paper if you need extra room to work.

3. Draw a picture, make a chart, or use symbols to help you solve.

4. Pay attention only to the important numbers in a problem.

5. Make sure you have performed the correct operation
   (+, –, x, or ÷).

6. Make sure you follow the order of operations.

7. Always show your work.

8. Read each answer choice before choosing.
   Then choose the best answer.

9. If you don't know a word, look it up or ask for help.

10. Always check your answer. Does it make sense?
    Does it answer the question?

Fill in a bubble like this: ●

not like this: ✗ ✓ ⊛

Skills and Concepts

Place Value

- identify place values to billions and thousandths
- interpret place-value charts
- identify place name and value of digits
- write numeral described by place names
- read/write numerals in expanded form
- name value of specified digit in a numeral

Geometry

- distinguish between two- and three-dimensional figures
- name 2- and 3-D figures
- match congruent and similar shapes and angles
- identify lines of symmetry
- determine inclusion in overlapping shapes
- match geometric prefixes with number of sides
- find perimeter and area

Word Problems

- solve word problems using addition, subtraction, multiplication, and division
- determine operations in multi-step problems
- exclude unnecessary information
- match solution sentences to given problem
- solve word problems using whole numbers, fractions, and decimals

Computation

- practice with basic addition, subtraction, multiplication, and division facts in a singular and mixed format
- perform 2+ digit addition, subtraction, and multiplication computations with/without regrouping

Place-Value Models/Fractions

- identify place-value models to thousands
- name the number shown by a model representation
- draw place-value models to represent a given number
- add and subtract using models with/without regrouping

Number Concepts

- write/match a solution sentence to pictured operation
- recognize fact families
- use the associative, commutative, and identity properties
- correlate addition and multiplication
- equalize multi-operational equations

Time/Money

- solve word problems with time and money
- identify coin values
- compute (+, −, x, ÷) with money
- find the amount of change due or tax involved
- express money values using $ and ¢
- create minimal collections of coins for given amounts
- interpret charts with money

Patterns/Probability

- continue a given pattern of shapes or numbers
- identify the missing element(s) in a pattern sequence
- supply a specified pattern element when the sequence immediately preceding is absent

Compare and Order Numbers

- identify or write numerical sets including decimals and fractions in order from least to greatest and vice versa with number values to billions and thousandths
- identify specific numbers in number order
- order chart information from least to greatest and vice versa

Measurement

- identify and use standard and metric units in measuring length, mass, volume, and temperature
- identify uses of measurement tools
- compare metric and standard units
- measure pictured objects within a ruled space
- measure with a nonstandard unit

Number Lines/Words

- locate numbers or a specific group of numbers on a number line
- identify missing numbers
- identify or create a number line to match a given picture or computation
- write or identify numbers or number words for given values or places to billions

Computation

- for added practice with computational skills as in row one
- for inclusion of reasonableness, estimation, or probability

Graphs/Tables

- interpret, combine, and compare chart data
- construct graphs given the chart data
- interpret and construct tally charts, picture graphs, bar graphs, point and line graphs, and pie graphs
- combine and compare data

Problem Solving

- use problem-solving strategies such as logical thinking, working backward, guess and check, and drawing a picture
- solve problems with multi-step and multi-informational components
- calculate missing variables by using given information

Estimation/Reasonableness

- round numbers to tens, hundreds, and thousands
- use front-end estimation or rounding to calculate sums, differences, products, and quotients
- choose a reasonable numerical value to match a given situation (time/money situations are also included here)

Repeated Practice

- for added practice with any skill/concept included on this page or in previous lessons

Note: Provisions for calculator use in exploring patterns, number concepts, problem solving, and estimation are indicated on the scope and sequence chart.

Skills and Concepts

Place Value (cont.)
- compare/order digits in numbers according to place value
- determine place value to which a number has been rounded

Geometry (cont.)
- label parallel, perpendicular, or intersecting lines
- count angles, vertices, faces, and edges of plane & solid figures
- identify hexagon, pentagon, polygon, prism, rhombus, parallelogram, trapezoid, quadrilateral, as well as equilateral, isosceles, and scalene triangles
- distinguish among flips, slides, and turns

Word Problems (cont.)
- identify information needed to solve a problem
- match solution sentences to given problem
- match common clue words to operations
- use concepts of time and money to solve problems
- use calculator to assist and verify solutions

Computation (cont.)
- divide 2+ digit numerals with/without remainders and with 1+ digit divisors
- compute using zeros in all operations
- add 2+ digit columns with/without regrouping
- check subtraction with addition and vice versa
- supply missing addends, multipliers, and divisors

Place Value Models/Fractions (cont.)
- use decimal representations for addition, subtraction, and multiplication
- identify fractional parts of shaded figures and or sets
- compare/equalize/simplify fractions with/without picture representation
- add, subtract, and multiply fractions and mixed numbers

Number Concepts (cont.)
- supply missing addends
- use non-equality in equations
- identify true and non-true equations
- calculate mean, median, range, and mode
- apply greatest common factor and least common multiple
- perform operations with exponents

Time/Money (cont.)
- determine comparative money values
- compute portion when given a set group value
- identify clock face time by hour, half-hour, and minute intervals
- determine elapsed time using clocks
- determine elapsed time in word problems

Patterns/Probability (cont.)
- describe the rule for a pattern sequence
- create a pattern using specified units
- visualize pattern to designated conclusion
- continue situational patterns
- investigate patterns with calculator

Compare and Order Numbers (cont.)
- use the inequality symbols > and < to compare numbers
- choose a group of numbers according to a specified order
- use odd and even numbers, skip counting, and number patterns in ordering
- compare and order units of standard and metric measurements

Measurement (cont.)
- compare given measurements
- use a ruler to measure the perimeter of given shapes
- estimate situational uses with the appropriate unit
- determine area, volume, and perimeter with/without all dimensions given
- find equivalent measurements
- use symmetry and congruence in calculating measurements
- enlarge to scale using grids

Number Lines/Words (cont.)
- match equations to number line representation
- locate representative points for fractions/decimals on a number line
- write or match words for fractions and decimals

Computation (cont.)
(see page 8)

Graphs/Tables (cont.)
- use symbols having a value of more than 1 unit and of half a unit
- write questions regarding a graph
- determine unit of comparison in a graph
- write concise summary of graph data
- plot number pairs
- give number pair location of a symbol on a grid

Problem Solving (cont.)
- choose possible solutions given indefinite variables
- select an amount large enough to include the combined variables given
- order objects or numbers in sequence given non-sequential variables
- write questions for given solutions regarding data available

Estimation/Reasonableness (cont.)
- round decimals to nearest hundredth, tenth, or whole number
- select equations for best estimate of given values
- visually estimate comparative sizes
- use calculations to verify estimations

Repeated Practice (cont.)
(see page 8)

Skills and Concepts

Place Value (cont.)

(see pages 8–9)

Geometry (cont.)

- select figures with specified characteristics
- classify right, acute, obtuse, and corresponding angles
- name by identifying points: line, segment, ray, chord, radius, diameter, and circumference

Word Problems (cont.)

- apply problem-solving strategies and concept development

Computation (cont.)

- add, subtract, and multiply fractions/mixed fractions
- add, subtract, multiply, and divide decimals to thousandths
- use calculator to verify computations

Place-Value Models/ Fractions (cont.)

- utilize common denominators in computations
- find ratios/equivalent ratios
- identify decimal values to thousandths
- compare decimals to fractional parts
- find equivalent decimals
- add, subtract, multiply, and divide decimals

Number Concepts (cont.)

- use order of operations in multi-computational equations
- label prime and composite numbers
- complete factor trees

Time/Money (cont.)

- recognize values of standard time units
- determine equivalent measures of time
- interpret schedules
- designate AM or PM

Patterns/Probability (cont.)

- choose possible outcomes or non-inclusion in a given set of conditions
- write probability in fractional terms
- compare probability in different sets and in multi-chance situations
- compute simple odds

Compare and Order Numbers (cont.)

(see pages 8–9)

Measurement (cont.)

- measure length, area, and perimeter using 1/2 units
- identify formulas for finding area and perimeter
- find area and circumference of circles

Number Lines/Words (cont.)

(see pages 8–9)

Computation (cont.)

(see page 8)

Graphs/Tables (cont.)

- determine number pair inclusion in overlapping shapes on a grid
- interpret calendars
- plot number pairs
- give number pair location of a symbol on a grid

Problem Solving (cont.)

- solve for n in equations
- complete logic problems using process of elimination
- classify according to given descriptors
- write questions for given solutions regarding data available

Estimation/ Reasonableness (cont.)

(see pages 8–9)

Repeated Practice (cont.)

(see page 8)

Scope and Sequence

Skills/Concepts	1	T	2	T	3	T	4	T	5	T	6	T	7	T	8	T	9	T	10	T	11	T	12	T	13	T	14	T	15	T	16	T	17	T	18	T	19	T	20	T
1 Place Value																																								
2 Geometry																																								
3 Word Problems																																								
4 Basic Facts																																								
5 Addition																																								
6 Subtraction																																								
7 Multiplication																																								
8 Division																																								
9 Place Value																																								
10 Fractions																																								
11 Decimals																																								
12 Number Concepts																																								
13 Time																																								
14 Money																																								
15 Patterns																																								
16 Compare/Order Numbers																																								
17 Measurement																																								
18 Number Lines																																								
19 Number Words																																								
20 Graphs/Tables																																								
21 Problem Solving																																								
22 Estimation																																								
23 Reasonableness																																								
24 Probability																																								
25 Repeated Practice/ Calculator Opportunity																																								

T = Weekly Test   • Indicates Skill or Concept Included and/or Tested

Scope and Sequence

Skills/Concepts	21	T	22	T	23	T	24	T	25	T	26	T	27	T	28	T	29	T	30	T	31	T	32	T	33	T	34	T	35	T	36	T	37	T	38	T	39	T	40	T
1 Place Value	•	•	•	•	•	•	•	•	•	•	•	•	•	•	•	•	•	•	•	•	•	•	•	•	•	•	•	•	•	•	•	•	•	•	•	•	•	•	•	•
2 Geometry	•	•	•	•	•	•	•		•	•	•	•	•	•	•	•	•	•	•	•	•	•	•	•	•	•	•	•	•	•	•	•	•	•	•	•	•	•	•	•
3 Word Problems	•	•	•	•	•	•		•	•	•	•	•	•	•	•	•	•	•	•	•	•	•	•	•	•	•	•	•	•	•	•	•	•	•	•	•	•	•	•	•
4 Basic Facts	•				•						•	•	•		•		•	•	•		•		•	•					•	•	•	•	•	•	•	•	•	•	•	•
5 Addition		•	•	•		•	•	•	•	•	•	•	•	•	•	•	•	•	•	•	•	•	•	•	•	•	•	•	•	•	•	•	•	•	•	•	•	•	•	•
6 Subtraction	•		•	•	•		•	•	•		•		•		•	•	•		•	•	•	•	•	•	•	•	•	•	•	•	•	•	•	•	•	•	•	•	•	•
7 Multiplication		•	•		•	•	•	•	•	•	•	•	•	•	•	•	•	•	•	•	•	•	•	•	•	•	•	•	•	•	•	•	•	•	•	•	•	•	•	•
8 Division				•			•		•						•		•		•	•	•		•		•		•	•	•	•	•	•	•	•	•	•	•	•	•	
9 Place Value	•	•	•	•	•	•	•	•	•	•	•	•	•	•	•	•	•	•	•	•	•	•	•	•	•	•	•	•	•	•	•	•	•	•	•	•	•	•	•	•
10 Fractions						•				•		•	•		•		•	•	•		•		•	•	•		•		•		•	•	•	•	•	•	•		•	
11 Decimals	•	•	•		•	•	•	•	•	•	•	•	•	•	•	•	•	•	•	•	•	•	•		•		•	•	•	•	•	•	•	•	•	•	•	•	•	•
12 Number Concepts									•			•	•		•	•	•	•	•		•	•	•	•	•	•	•	•	•	•	•	•	•	•	•	•	•	•	•	•
13 Time	•		•	•	•		•		•	•	•		•		•	•	•		•			•	•				•		•		•		•			•	•		•	•
14 Money	•		•	•			•		•		•	•			•		•		•	•	•	•	•	•	•	•	•	•	•	•	•	•	•	•	•		•		•	•
15 Patterns								•				•			•			•		•	•		•		•	•	•	•	•	•	•	•	•		•	•	•	•		•
16 Compare/Order Numbers	•	•									•		•				•				•				•		•		•		•		•	•	•	•	•	•	•	•
17 Measurement	•	•	•	•	•	•	•	•	•		•	•	•	•	•	•	•		•	•	•	•	•	•	•	•	•	•	•	•	•	•	•	•	•	•	•	•	•	•
18 Number Lines	•	•	•		•				•				•				•		•				•								•		•				•		•	•
19 Number Words	•							•		•	•		•								•										•		•	•	•		•		•	
20 Graphs/Tables	•	•	•	•	•		•		•		•		•		•		•		•		•	•	•	•	•		•	•	•	•	•	•	•	•	•	•	•	•	•	•
21 Problem Solving	•	•	•	•	•	•	•	•	•	•	•	•	•	•	•	•	•	•	•	•	•		•	•	•	•	•	•	•	•	•	•	•	•	•	•	•	•	•	•
22 Estimation	•	•	•	•	•	•	•	•	•	•	•		•		•		•	•	•	•	•	•	•	•	•	•	•	•	•	•	•	•	•	•	•	•	•	•	•	
23 Reasonableness																																		•		•				
24 Probability	•	•	•						•		•	•	•						•		•								•		•									
25 Repeated Practice/Calculator Opportunity									•							•	•															•							•	

T = Weekly Test   • Indicates Skill or Concept Included and/or Tested

How many digits are needed to create a number in the

hundred millions

_____

ten thousands

_____

hundreds _____

Which shape has two lines of symmetry? _____

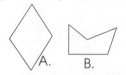

Hannah completed 4 pages of homework every day for 7 days. How many pages of homework did she complete in all? _____

Subtract. Check by adding.

3,000
− 2,971

Write the fraction for the shaded part of each shape.

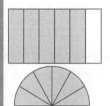

___

___

$5 \times (8 + 2) = (5 \times 8)$
$+ (5 \times \_\_\_) = \boxed{}$

$3 \times (7 + 1) = (3 \times 7)$
$+ (3 \times \_\_\_) = \boxed{}$

Using the least number of the coins below, show how to make $1.74.

_____ quarters

_____ dimes

_____ nickels

_____ pennies

31, 28, 25, 22

The formula for the pattern above is

○ add 3

○ subtract 3

○ count by 5s

○ subtract 2

What number is 1,000 more than 9,235?

○ 9,335

○ 8,235

○ 10,235

○ 11,235

What is the perimeter of the figure below?

_____ units

What is the area?

_____ square units

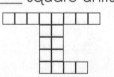

Write the number word for

2,000,405 _____

_____

_____

610,240 _____

_____

$9 \times 8 =$ _____

$8 \times 7 =$ _____

$7 \times 6 =$ _____

$9 \times 7 =$ _____

$8 \times 4 =$ _____

Write >, <, or = to describe the information in this graph.

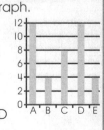

A ☐ D

E ☐ C

D ☐ B

Mystery Numbers

$A = B \times 3$

$B = D - 10$

$C =$ the sum of 7 and 3

$D = C + C$

$A =$ _____ $B =$ _____

$C =$ _____ $D =$ _____

Estimate the sum by rounding to the tens place.

2,832
1,179
6,208
+ 4,385

●▲▲▲▲■■

The above shapes are in a sack. With one draw, the chances of drawing a ▲ would be

_____ out of _____

Assessment

1 Subtract. Check by adding.

7,000
− 6,294

2

6 x 7 = _____

8 x 9 = _____

4 x 8 = _____

7 x 8 = _____

3 Estimate the sum by rounding to the tens place.

4,351
4,174
3,233
+ 5,155

4 Nate was at summer camp for 9 days. He went fishing each day. If he caught 6 fish every day, how many fish did he catch while he was at camp? _____

5

6 x (4 + 5) = (6 x 4) + (6 x _____) = ▢

5 x (2 + 7) = (5 x 2) + (5 x _____) = ▢

6 Which number is 1,000 less than 10,247?

○ 9,247

○ 11,237

○ 10,357

○ 9,147

7 How many digits are needed to create a number in the

hundred thousands_____

ten millions _____

thousands_____

8 Which figure has two lines of symmetry? _____

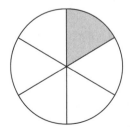

A.   B.   C.

9 Using the least number of the coins below, show how to make $2.49.

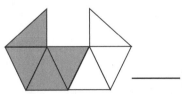

_____   _____   _____   _____
quarters   dimes   nickels   pennies

10 Write the fraction for the shaded part of each figure.

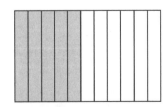

_____   _____   _____

0-7682-3205-8 *Math 4 Today*

Write the numbers with the following place values.

eight ten thousands, five hundreds, two tens, seven ones

_____

six hundred millions, two hundred thousands, one thousand, nine tens, four ones

_____

Shade the figures that have dotted lines showing the lines of symmetry.

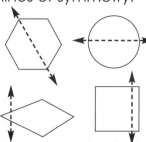

Mr. Know has 24 students in his science class. He would like to have 4 students at each table. How many tables will he need for his class?

_____

---

9 x 9 = _____

8 x 8 = _____

7 x 7 = _____

6 x 6 = _____

5 x 5 = _____

Day #1

Write the equivalent fractions.

_____ = _____

_____ = _____

Write the fact family for 7, 8, and 56.

_____

_____

_____

_____

Kim began her piano practice at 4:20. She practiced for 35 minutes. At what time did she stop practicing?

_____

Which equation describes the pattern?

○ n + n

○ n x n

○ n – n

○ n + 2

Day #2

Which number is less than 11,437 and more than 10,992?

○ 10,990

○ 11,532

○ 10,005

○ 11,235

What is the perimeter of the figure below?

_____cm

What is the area?

_____ sq. cm

8 cm

6 cm

Write the number word.

15,320,100_____

_____

_____

350,205,500 _____

_____

_____

---

16 ÷ 2 = _____

25 ÷ 5 = _____

8 ÷ 4 = _____

12 ÷ 3 = _____

15 ÷ 3 = _____

Day #3

Gymnastic Meet Total Scores	
Christy	35
Alicia	40
Leyla	25
Kalyn	50

On the back of this paper, draw a bar graph to describe the data in the chart with 1 bar = 5. Write three summary statements.

Mystery Numbers

A = B x 7

B = 12 ÷ 3

C = D – A

D = A + B

A = _____ B = _____

C = _____ D = _____

Dennis bought a game for $27.50, a book for $6.25, a model kit for $14.95, and a shirt for $22.99. About how much money did he spend?

○ $71.00

○ $85.00

○ $100.00

○ $92.00

Match.

_____ 10 centimeters

_____ 100 centimeters

_____ 10 decimeters

_____ 1,000 meters

A. kilometer

B. meter

C. decimeter

Day #4

0-7682-3205-8 *Math 4 Today*

Assessment

1

$16 \div 8 =$ _____

$18 \div 2 =$ _____

$25 \div 5 =$ _____

$15 \div 3 =$ _____

2

$6 \times 6 =$ _____

$8 \times 8 =$ _____

$4 \times 4 =$ _____

$9 \times 9 =$ _____

3

20	18	16	14
10	9	8	7

The equation for this pattern is

◯ $n + 5$

◯ $n - 4$

◯ $n \div 2$

4 Write each number word.

251,718,400 _____

_____

_____

62,502,194 _____

_____

_____

5 Kala has 35 stickers to give to each of her 5 friends. How many stickers will she give each friend if each one gets the same number of stickers?

_____

6

100s on the Spelling Tests

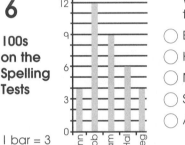

1 bar = 3

Which statements are true for this graph?

◯ Bob > Meg

◯ Hal > Sam

◯ Meg = Ann

◯ Sam = 9

◯ Ann + Meg + Hal = Bob

7 Margo and Patsy went to see a play. The play began at 3:20 and lasted for 45 minutes. At what time did the play end? _____

8 What is the perimeter of the figure?

_____ cm

What is the area?

_____ sq. cm

7 cm

4 cm

9 Write the number made up of each of the following place values.

six hundred thousands, eight thousands, nine hundreds, zero tens, seven ones

_____

_____

10 Heidi was doing chores to earn money. She earned $7.54 during the first week of November. She earned $32.99 during the second week, $12.50 the third week, and $24.95 the last week of the month. About how much money did Heidi earn during November?

◯ $100.00

◯ $85.00

◯ $66.00

◯ $79.00

Fill in the missing digits.

seven hundred sixty-two million, nine hundred forty-five thousand, two hundred fifty-eight

7___2,___ ___5,___ ___8

Match.

line XY ___

line segment XY ___

ray XY ___

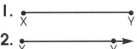

1. •————•
    X   Y

2. •————•→
    X   Y

3. ←•————•→
    X   Y

Ms. Rye has 12 roses, 18 daisies, and 3 vases. She wants an equal number of roses and an equal number of daisies in each vase. Show how to find the number of roses and daisies she will put in each vase.

_____

---

9 x 6 = _____

8 x 5 = _____

9 x 8 = _____

8 x 7 = _____

9 x 4 = _____

Shade in the second figure in each pair to complete the equivalent fractions. Fill in the second fraction.

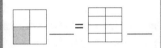

Which pair are NOT related facts?

○ 8 x 9 = 72
  72 ÷ 9 - 8

○ 6 x 6 = 36
  6 - 6 = 0

○ 8 x 4 = 32
  4 x 8 = 32

○ 7 x 5 = 35
  35 ÷ 5 = 7

The Hampton family arrived at their grandparents' home at 6:40 Sunday evening. The drive had taken 1 hour and 10 minutes. At what time did the Hamptons leave home?_____

1, 6, 4, 9, 7, 12, 10, 15, 13, 18, 16, 21

What is the rule for the above pattern?

_____

_____

Which number is more than 125,437, but less than 220,151?

○ 110,790

○ 251,031

○ 100,005

○ 211,835

What is the perimeter of the figure below?

_____ units

What is the area?

_____ square units

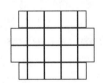

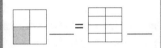

0 1 2 3 4 5 6 7 8 9 10 11 12 13 14 15

This number line shows

○ 14 - 9 = 5

○ 7 + 8 = 15

○ 14 ÷ 7 = 2

○ 7 x 7 = 49

---

18 ÷ 3 = _____

24 ÷ 6 = _____

27 ÷ 9 = _____

36 ÷ 6 = _____

20 ÷ 4 = _____

Student Spelling Stars

Kira	★★★★★
Mike	★★★
Lance	★★★★★★
Deb	★

each ★ = 6 A+ tests

What is the total number of A+ spelling tests shown on this graph? _____

Max is older than Ivan. Hal is younger than Ivan but older than Greg.

Which statements could be true?

○ Max is older than Hal.

○ Ivan is younger than Greg.

○ Hal is the youngest.

○ Greg is younger than Max.

Quaid picked 82 bushels of apples on Monday and 91 bushels on Tuesday. Carmen picked 52 bushels on Wednesday and 75 bushels on Thursday. About how many more bushels of apples did Quaid pick?

○ 70   ○ 40

○ 20   ○ 100

---

10 centimeters = 1 decimeter

It takes 8 decimeters of shipping paper to wrap a large package for mailing. How many centimeters of paper would be needed?

_____

Assessment

1

20 ÷ 5 = _____

18 ÷ 6 = _____

24 ÷ 4 = _____

27 ÷ 3 = _____

2

4 x 9 = _____

7 x 8 = _____

8 x 9 = _____

6 x 9 = _____

3 Eva read 22 pages on Monday and 91 pages on Tuesday. Mario read 89 pages on Monday and 63 pages on Tuesday. About how many more pages did Mario read?

○ 20   ○ 50

○ 40   ○ 90

4 Juan has 48 stamps and 36 stickers. He wants to glue the same number of stamps and the same number of stickers onto 6 pages in his collector's album. Show how to find the total number of stamps and stickers he will put on each page.

5 Which pair are NOT related facts?

○ 8 x 8 = 64   64 ÷ 8 = 8

○ 8 + 8 = 16   8 – 8 = 0

○ 4 x 6 = 24   6 x 4 = 24

○ 5 x 9 = 45   45 ÷ 9 = 5

6 Which numbers are more than 347,129 but less than 412,076?

○ 418,000   ○ 398,899

○ 409,778   ○ 362,901

○ 447,202   ○ 332,388

○ 4,001,033   ○ 34,100

7 Fill in the missing digits for each number.

nine hundred eighty-six thousand, four hundred thirty-five

9___ ___,___3___

seven hundred twenty-one thousand, two hundred ninety-eight

___ ___ 1,___ ___ 8

8 Match.

_____ line AB

_____ ray AB

_____ line segment AB

_____ ray YX

_____ line segment XY

1. X————————Y

2. A←————————→B

3. X←————————Y

4. A————————→B

5. A•————————•B

9 A new play is opening in the city. It begins at 8:00. It takes Carol's family 1 hour and 25 minutes to drive to the city. At what time should Carol's family leave home in order to arrive at the play on time? _____

10 Shade in the second figure to complete the equivalent fraction.

____ = ____

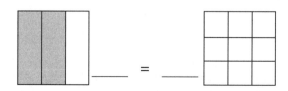

____ = ____

Name

Day #1

Write in expanded form.

two hundred ninety-one thousand, eight hundred fifteen

_____

_____

_____

_____

Match.
A. ray   B. line
C. line segment

_____ a straight figure with two end points

_____ a straight figure, with no end points, that extends forever in both directions

_____ a straight figure, with one end point, that extends forever in one direction

Holly displays her 54 music boxes on 6 shelves in her room. She also keeps 12 dolls on the shelves. If she arranges the music boxes and the dolls equally, how many items are on each shelf? _____

$$34 \times 2 \qquad 43 \times 3$$

$$51 \times 5 \qquad 52 \times 4$$

Day #2

Shade in the second figure to complete the equivalent fraction.

  =

  =

A common factor of 4 and 8 is 2 because 2 x 2 = 4 and 2 x 4 = 8.

Other than 1, what are common factors for these number pairs.

10 and 15 _____

12 and 21 _____

7 and 14 _____

Name the coins and the amount needed for change.

Cost   Amount Given
$0.79 $1.00
Change _____

_____

Cost   Amount Given
$0.37 $0.50
Change _____

_____

2, 4, 7, 14, 17, 34, 37, 74, 77, 154

What is the rule for the above pattern?

_____

_____

Day #3

Mountain	Feet in Height
Annapuma	26,504
Kilimanjaro	19,340
Dap Sang	28,250
Everest	29,028
Cho Oyu	26,750

List the mountains in order of height from least to greatest.

_____

_____

_____

_____

What is perimeter of the figure below?

_____ units
What is the area?
_____ square units

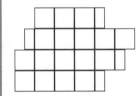

This number line shows

○ 15 ÷ 5 = 3

○ 7 + 8 = 15

○ 5 ÷ 5 = 1

○ 5 x 5 = 25

49 ÷ 7 = _____

54 ÷ 6 = _____

63 ÷ 9 = _____

72 ÷ 8 = _____

81 ÷ 9 = _____

Day #4

Hours of TV Watched per Month

Room 401 ☐☐

Room 402 ☐☐☐☐

Room 403 ☐☐☐☐☐

each ☐ = 25 hours

How many more hours of TV were watched by Room 403 than Room 401?_____

Ann read fewer books than Susan. Linda read more books than Ann, but fewer than Tammy. Which statements could be true?

○ Ann read the least number of books.

○ Tammy read the most.

○ Linda read more books than Tammy.

Todd earned the following amounts last summer.

June	$57.98
July	$92.33
August	$66.88

About how much money did Todd earn last summer?

○ $220   ○ $250

○ $300   ○ $120

10 decimeters = 1 meter

Sam measured 8 meters to make a pen for his pet rabbits. At the store, the fencing he wanted for the pen was sold only in decimeters. How many decimeters of fencing would he need to buy? _____

Assessment

1

$63 \div 7 =$ _____

$72 \div 9 =$ _____

$54 \div 9 =$ _____

$49 \div 7 =$ _____

2

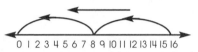

$\begin{array}{c} 43 \\ \times\ 2 \\ \hline \end{array}$ $\begin{array}{c} 63 \\ \times\ 3 \\ \hline \end{array}$ $\begin{array}{c} 12 \\ \times\ 4 \\ \hline \end{array}$

3 What is the rule for this pattern?

1, 3, 2, 6, 5, 15, 14, 42, 41

_____

4

0 1 2 3 4 5 6 7 8 9 10 11 12 13 14 15 16

This number line shows

◯ 8 + 8 = 16   ◯ 16 ÷ 2 = 8

◯ 8 x 8 = 64   ◯ 8 – 8 = 0

5 Marcus is setting the table for his party. He has invited 8 guests. For party favors, he bought 24 balloons and 16 candy bars. How many party favors will he set at each place if each guest gets an equal number of balloons and candy bars? _____

6 Students Wearing Glasses.   each b = 30 students

Grade			Grade	
A. Third	bbbb		**B.** Third	bbb
Fourth	bbb		Fourth	bbbbbb
Fifth	bbbbb		Fifth	bbbbbbb
Sixth	bbbbb		Sixth	b

Which graph shows that 90 more students in fifth grade wear glasses than the students in fourth grade? _____

7 Name the coins and amounts needed for change.

Cost $5.49   Amount Given $6.00

_____

_____

Cost $3.22   Amount Given $4.12

_____

_____

8 What is the perimeter and the area of the figure below?

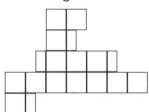

perimeter = _____ units

area = _____ square units

9 Write the number in expanded form.

seven hundred ninety-two thousand, six hundred five

_____

_____

10 The chart shows the number of long distance calls made by the School Computer Supply Company for the fall months of 2002.

Month	Number of Calls
September	297
October	341
November	196

About how many calls were made by the company during these months?

◯ 700   ◯ 900

◯ 600   ◯ 800

0-7682-3205-8 *Math 4 Today*

Day #1

400,000 + 90,000 + 3,000 + 500 + 7 =
- ○ forty-nine thousand, three hundred fifty-seven
- ○ four hundred nine thousand, three thousand seven
- ○ four hundred ninety-three thousand, five hundred seven

Which show right angles?

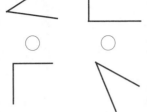

○   ○

○   ○

James is making collages for his 4 aunts. For decoration, he wants to put 6 leaves, 4 shells, and 3 flowers on each collage. How many decorations will he need to make all the collages?

_____

44	13
x 5	x 7

58	29
x 5	x 4

Day #2

Shade in $\frac{1}{3}$ of each set.

A common factor of 4 and 8 is 2 because 2 x 2 = 4 and 2 x 4 = 8.

Other than 1, what are common factors for these number pairs.

27 and 18 _____

30 and 40 _____

35 and 21 _____

Name the bills, coins, and amount needed for change.

Cost	Amount Given
$3.81	$5.00

Change _____

_____

Cost	Amount Given
$7.17	$10.00

Change _____

_____

Continue the pattern.

45	42	39	36
15	14	13	12

33		
11		

Day #3

Write the odd numbers between 3,497 and 3,511.

_____

_____

_____

_____

_____

Mrs. Thomas drove from Dallas, Texas to Ft. Worth, Texas. She traveled about
- ○ 55 kilograms
- ○ 55 liters
- ○ 55 kilometers
- ○ 55 decimeters

Write AM or PM.

Julio's party begins at 3:00. _____

The school tardy bell rings at 8:15. _____

The toy store opens at 9:30. _____

The evening news comes on at 6:00. ____

9 x _____ = 72

3 x _____ = 27

_____ x 4 = 32

_____ x 7 = 63

Day #4

City Science Fair

School	Solar System Projects
Dayton	★★★★✦
Ryan	★★★
Adly	★★★★★★
Marcus	★✦

each ★ = 4

How many solar system projects were entered in the science fair? ____

Tyesha and Eric together have 29 posters. Eric has 7 more posters than Tyesha. How many posters does each student have?

_____

_____

Estimate the difference by rounding to the hundreds place.

2,359	7,944
– 1,231	– 5,679

1,000 meters = 1 kilometer

Tam and Isaac walked 2 and $\frac{1}{2}$ kilometers along a hiking trail. How many meters did they walk? _____

Assessment

1

9 x _____ = 63

8 x _____ = 32

_____ x 9 = 27

_____ x 9 = 72

2

29	38	69
x 2	x 4	x 3

3 Estimate the difference by rounding to the hundreds place.

8,712
− 4,189

4 Mrs. Wong is making centerpieces for 7 tables. She wants to put 8 daisies, 7 carnations, and 5 roses in each centerpiece. How many flowers will she need? _____

5 What is a common factor for each pair of numbers?

45 and 10 _____

81 and 72 _____

36 and 30 _____

6 Write the even numbers between 5,996 and 6,010.

_____   _____

_____   _____

_____   _____

7 600,000 + 70,000 + 2,000 + 10 + 4 =

○ six hundred seventy-two thousand, fourteen

○ six hundred seven thousand, two hundred fourteen

○ sixty-seven million, two thousand, one hundred four

8 Lilly's family left home from Dallas, Texas for a ski trip in Denver, Colorado. About how far did they travel?

○ 1,200 grams

○ 1,200 centimeters

○ 1,200 kilometers

○ 1,200 meters

9 Write AM or PM.

Raul's parents went to a late movie. They returned home at 11:30. _____

Cindy had a piano lesson after school. Her lesson started at 4:30. _____

Gerald's dad took an early flight. His plane left at 7:30. _____

10 Shade in $\frac{1}{5}$ of each set.

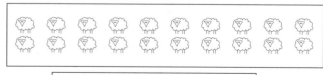

Day # 1

What is the value of the 5 in each number?

3,458,201 _____

152,670,400

_____

61,250 _____

Which show acute angles?

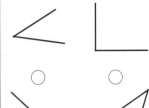

At Midland Elementary, there are 22 students in each of 7 fourth-grade classes. How many students are in fourth-grade at Midland? _____

$\begin{array}{r} 17 \\ \times\ 10 \\ \hline \end{array}$ $\begin{array}{r} 23 \\ \times\ 10 \\ \hline \end{array}$

$\begin{array}{r} 84 \\ \times\ 10 \\ \hline \end{array}$ $\begin{array}{r} 33 \\ \times\ 10 \\ \hline \end{array}$

Day # 2

Shade in $\frac{2}{6}$ of each set.

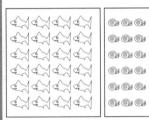

Other than 1, what are the common factors for these number pairs?

24 and 12 _____

_____ _____ _____

10 and 30 _____

_____ _____

What time will the clock show in 2 hours and 15 minutes? _____

What figure would come next in this pattern?

○ ⬭

○ ⬡

○ ⟋⟍

Day # 3

145,298 ☐ ☐ 167,109

Which two numbers could go in the empty boxes?

○ 168,231 169,345

○ 142,789 234,188

○ 14,388 15,632

○ 156,954 162,599

Mr. Valdez was loading stones to put into a wheelbarrow. The wheelbarrow can carry the weight of about

○ 80 grams

○ 80 kilograms

○ 80 kilometers

○ 80 centimeters

Write the number using numerals for seven hundred eighty-six million, four hundred two thousand, five hundred ninety-one

_____

$\begin{array}{r} 100 \\ \times\ 15 \\ \hline \end{array}$ $\begin{array}{r} 100 \\ \times\ 46 \\ \hline \end{array}$

$\begin{array}{r} 100 \\ \times\ 72 \\ \hline \end{array}$ $\begin{array}{r} 100 \\ \times\ 93 \\ \hline \end{array}$

Day # 4

What is the difference between the number of points scored by Mark and the number of points scored by Hank? _____

Volleyball Tournament Points

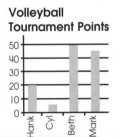

Judy and Ramey together have 42 stuffed animals. Judy has 12 fewer animals than Ramey. How many stuffed animals does each girl have? _____

_____

Lynn's Reading Chart

Monday	36 pages
Tuesday	42 pages
Wednesday	39 pages
Thursday	0 pages

How could you estimate the total number of pages Lynn read?

○ 42 ÷ 4   ○ 40 x 3

○ 42 – 39   ○ 20 x 4

In a deck of 52 cards, there are 2 jokers and 4 each of the number cards, 1–10. The probability of picking a joker is 2 out of 52 or $\frac{2}{52}$. Write, as a fraction, the probability of drawing a number 7 card. _____

Assessment

1

85   79
x 10   x 10

2

100   100
x 51   x 62

3

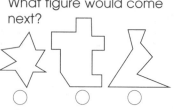

What figure would come next?

○   ○   ○

4 Write each number.

seventy-nine million, three hundred twenty-nine thousand, five hundred forty _____

four hundred ten million, three thousand, one hundred eighty-two

_____

5 There are 9 photographs on each page of a travel book. The book has 67 pages. How many photographs are in the book? _____

6 What is the difference between the pounds of paper recycled by Max and the pounds of paper recycled by Lou? _____

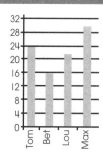

7 In art class, Kaly and Nate together painted 33 pictures during the year. Kaly painted 9 fewer pictures than Nate. How many pictures did each child paint? _____

8 Label each angle.

RA = right angle   AA = acute angle

___ ___ ___ ___ ___

9 What is the value of the 3 in each number?

321,890,267 _____

889,032,901 _____

3,290,177,200 _____

10

Basketball Goals for the Season

Ty	17
Jamal	23
Pete	24
Kito	2
Nino	21

How could you estimate the number of goals made by all the boys?

○ 23 + 24 + 17

○ 4 x 20

○ 5 x 20

○ 5 x 25

○ 25 – 5

Day #1

What is the value of the 2 in each number?

9,468,201

_____

752,610,400

_____

21,390 _____

_____

Which show obtuse angles?

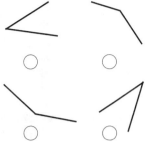

○   ○

○   ○

If there are 365 days in one year, how many days are in 7 years?

_____

37
x 30

54
x 40

Day #2

$\frac{1}{6}$ of 48 = _____

$\frac{1}{8}$ of 40 = _____

$\frac{1}{2}$ of 10 = _____

List the common factors for these number pairs. Circle the greatest common factor for each pair.

40 and 8 _____

_____

36 and 24 _____

_____

What time did the clock show 2 hours and 20 minutes ago? _____

Draw the sixth box in this pattern.

Day #3

100,051 ☐ ☐ 99,109

Which two numbers could go in the empty boxes?

○ 105,231   109,345

○ 906,789   902,188

○ 99,838   99,632

○ 98,054   93,107

Sandy made a jug of lemonade to serve 5 friends. About how much lemonade did she make?

○ 3 meters

○ 3 grams

○ 3 liters

○ 3 milliliters

Write each number

six million, twenty-two thousand, four hundred eighty-seven

_____

twenty-five million, three hundred seventeen thousand, fifty-nine

_____

357   652
x   8   x   7

229   934
x   5   x   3

Day #4

Write each number pair.

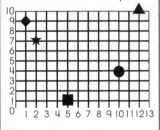

■ _____   ▲ _____

◆ _____   ● _____

★ _____

Mother needs to buy paper cups for 42 people. Which 2 packages could she buy to have enough paper cups without too many left over?

____ and ____

A.   B.   C.   D.

Four hundred seventy-two people bought concert tickets for $21.05 each. Which would be a way to estimate how much money was paid for the tickets?

○ 400 x $20 = $8,000

○ 500 x $20 = $10,000

○ 470 + $20 = $4970

○ 500 – $25 = $475

●●○○○○○

If these marbles are placed in a bag and one is drawn out, what is the probability that it will be white? _____

What is the probability that it will be black? _____

1

```
  95        62
x 50      x 80
```

2

```
  498       873
x   7     x   7
```

3 While on vacation, the Carter family drove 337 miles a day for 16 days. How could you estimate the number of miles they drove?

○ 300 x 20 = 6,000
○ 400 x 20 = 8,000
○ 337 – 16 = 321
○ 300 + 20 = 320

4 There are 168 hours in 1 week. How many hours are in 9 weeks? _____

5 List the common factors for these number pairs. Circle the greatest common factor.

64 and 16 _____ _____ _____

40 and 8 _____ _____ _____

6 Which two numbers could go in the empty boxes?

103,032 ☐ ☐ 100,091

○ 101,977   99,090
○ 104,234   100,459
○ 99,821   98,305
○ 100,621   100,243

7 What is the value of the 9 in each number?

391,820,267 _____

889,032,501 _____

3,270,179,200 _____

8 Label the angles.
RA = right angle AA = acute angle
OA = obtuse angle

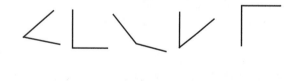

___ ___ ___ ___

9 What time did the clock show 4 hours and 20 minutes ago? _____

10

$\frac{1}{7}$ of 49 = _____

$\frac{1}{4}$ of 20 = _____

$\frac{1}{9}$ of 36 = _____

Day #1

Which number shows 7 thousands, 4 hundreds, 6 tens, and 18 ones?

○ 76,418

○ 74,618

○ 7,478

Which figures are polygons?

Marly's Country Store has 20 gumdrops in each of 6 candy jars. Which method could be used to find the total number of gumdrops?

○ add 20 and 6

○ multiply 20 by 6

○ subtract 6 from 20

○ divide 20 by 6

$$500 \times 28 \qquad 300 \times 56$$

Day #2

$\frac{1}{5}$ of 25 = _____

$\frac{1}{3}$ of 33 = _____

$\frac{1}{7}$ of 56 = _____

A. sum   B. difference
C. quotient D. product

_____ the answer to a division problem

_____ the answer to an addition problem

_____ the answer to a subtraction problem

_____ the answer to a multiplication problem

Kyle bought 6 new model kits. Each kit cost $8.79. How much money did Kyle spend on model kits? _____

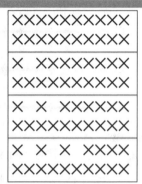

How many Xs will be in the tenth box? _____

Day #3

President	Term Served
Harry Truman	1945–1953
James Monroe	1817–1825
John Tyler	1841–1845
Herbert Hoover	1929–1933
John Adams	1797–1801

List the Presidents in order beginning with the earliest term to the most recent. _____

_____

_____

_____

_____

A. 9 kilograms
B. 3 meters
C. 2 grams
D. 300 liters
E. 20 milliliters
F. 1,500 kilograms
G. 80 kilograms

Which is the best estimate of mass for a

car _____
sack of groceries _____
pencil _____
TV _____

Which number line shows the whole numbers that are greater than 4 and less than 10? _____

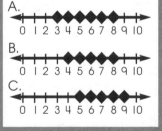

$3\overline{)14}$

$5\overline{)19}$

Day #4

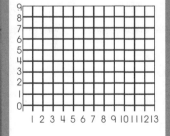

Plot these number pairs.

(11, 9)   (3, 0)

(13, 4)   (1, 8)

To decorate 5 dozen cupcakes with red hot candies, Nan needs about 550 red hots. Which 2 sacks of candy would be the best buy? _____

_____

353   177

255   379

Nine hundred thirty-seven people are seated at 28 tables for a banquet. How could you find the best estimate of the number of people at each table?

○ 900 ÷ 30 = 30

○ 900 x 20 = 18,000

○ 1,000 – 28 = 972

○ 1,000 ÷ 20 = 50

If these marbles are placed in a bag and one is drawn out, what is the probability that it will be white or black? _____

_____

Assessment

1

$$900 \quad\quad 600$$
$$\underline{\times\ 13} \quad\quad \underline{\times\ 72}$$

2

$4\overline{)27}$ $8\overline{)70}$

3 □□□○○○◆

If these shapes are in a bag, what is the probability (expressed as a fraction) of drawing a ◆ or a □ ?

_____

4 Which number line shows the numbers that are less than 12 and more than 5? _____

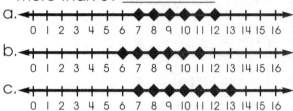

a.
b.
c.

5 Zeke packs 45 cans in each box. Today he packed 35 boxes. What method could be used to find the number of cans Zeke packed today?

○ add 45 and 35

○ multiply 45 by 35

○ subtract 35 from 45

6 Graph the number pairs.

(9, 11)

(3, 6)

(0, 10)

(7, 5)

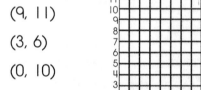

7 Ms. Silva needs to buy napkins for her company's picnic. She needs 715 napkins. Which 2 packages would be the best buy?

____ and ____

256   395   125   500

8 What is the best estimate of mass for

a pumpkin _____   a bus _____

a football _____   a spoon _____

A. 2,000 kilograms   B. 2,000 kilometers
C. 10 grams   D. 10 liters
E. 15 meters   F. 15 kilograms
G. 2 milliliters   H. 2 kilograms

9 Which number shows 56 thousands, 2 hundreds, 37 tens, and 8 ones?

○ 562,378

○ 56,378

○ 56,578

○ 56,478

10 Eight hundred fifteen new compact disks arrived at the music store. The disks are put on display racks in groups of 52. How could you find the best estimate of the number of display racks needed for the compact disks?

○ 800 x 50 = 40,000

○ 900 x 60 = 54,000

○ 800 + 50 = 850

○ 800 ÷ 50 = 16

Day #1

Which number shows 8 thousands, 4 hundreds, 11 tens, and 6 ones?

○ 8,411

○ 8,516

○ 9,116

Which letter is inside the square and circle but not inside the rectangle? _____

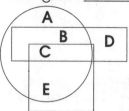

Hannah was baking a cherry pie for 8 of her friends. She had a carton of 241 cherries. When she finished the pie, Hannah had 17 cherries left. How many cherries did she use in the pie?

_____

```
 200      400
x  41    x  12
```

Day #2

Write each fraction in its simplest form.

$\frac{2}{4} =$ _____

$\frac{3}{9} =$ _____

$\frac{5}{15} =$ _____

Multiples are numbers made by multiplying a number by another number. For example, multiples of 5 are 5, 10, 15, 20...
List three multiples for each number.

3 _____, _____, _____

7 _____, _____, _____

9 _____, _____, _____

This clock shows about

○ 5:55   ○ 11:35

○ 11:20   ○ 11:27

```
0000000000000
0000000000000
000000000000
000000000000
00000000000
00000000000
```

How many 0's will be in the sixth box?

_____ 0's

Day #3

Write > or < to compare.

$\frac{1}{8}$ ☐ $\frac{1}{3}$

$\frac{1}{2}$ ☐ $\frac{1}{10}$

$\frac{1}{4}$ ☐ $\frac{1}{12}$

Which is the best estimate for the length of a

paper clip _____
dining table _____
bandage _____
railroad route _____
scissors _____

A. centimeter
B. decimeter
C. meter
D. kilometer

Write each number word.

$\frac{2}{8}$ _____

$\frac{5}{7}$ _____

$\frac{1}{2}$ _____

```
*******
*****      ____
*****     5)17

XXXXX
XXXXX
XXXXX     ____
XX        3)17
```

Day #4

January						
1	2	3	4	5	6	
7	8	9	10	11	12	13
14	15	16	17	18	19	20
21	22	23	24	25	26	27
28	29	30	31			

Which weeks have the greatest number of odd numbers? _____

Which weeks have the greatest number of even numbers? _____

Eve's number is greater than 15. Dan's number is not evenly divisible by 2. Meg's number is more than Eve's. Ken's number is a prime number.

	15	16	17	18
Eve				
Dan				
Meg				
Ken				

Six hundred twenty-one people bought tickets to the community theater's production of Pinocchio. The tickets cost $4.00 each. Which is the best estimate of the total ticket sales?

○ $1,400

○ $2,400

○ $3,400

A ☐ ▲ ▲ ● ■

B ☐ ▲ ● ■ ○

If these shapes are placed in a box and one is drawn out, which box, A or B, would give the best chance of drawing a ○? _____

1

$$
\begin{array}{r}
100 \\
\times\ 43 \\
\end{array}
\qquad
\begin{array}{r}
300 \\
\times\ 15 \\
\end{array}
$$

2

$5\overline{)18}$ $4\overline{)17}$

```
+ + + + +        * * * *
+ + + + +        * * * *
+ + + + +        * * * *
+ + +            * * * *
                 *
```

3 Four hundred seventy-nine people attended the Brigham School's Winter Festival. Each person paid $8.00 for a ticket. About how much did the school make from ticket sales?

- ○ $4,000
- ○ $5,000
- ○ $6,000
- ○ $7,000

4 At a sleepover, Karen and 12 of her friends toasted marshmallows in the fireplace. There were 161 marshmallows in 2 bags. When the girls finished, there were 39 marshmallows left over. How many marshmallows did they toast? _____

5 List three multiples for each number.

8 _____, _____, _____

2 _____, _____, _____

6 Write > or < to compare.

$\dfrac{1}{10}$ ☐ $\dfrac{1}{8}$ $\dfrac{1}{5}$ ☐ $\dfrac{1}{12}$

$\dfrac{1}{4}$ ☐ $\dfrac{1}{2}$ $\dfrac{1}{16}$ ☐ $\dfrac{1}{2}$

7 Which number shows 3 thousands, 9 hundreds, 17 tens, and 2 ones?

- ○ 4,072
- ○ 3,979
- ○ 4,172
- ○ 5,721

8 Which letter is inside the square and rectangle but not inside the circle?

_____

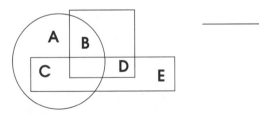

9 This clock shows about

- ○ 2:00
- ○ 2:30
- ○ 2:45
- ○ 2:53

10

February					
1	2	3	4	5	6
7	8	9	10	11	12	13
14	15	16	17	18	19	20
21	22	23	24	25	26	27
28					

Which week(s) have the greatest number of even numbers? _____

Which week(s) have the greatest number of odd numbers? _____

Day #1

Which number shows 17 hundreds, 3 tens, and 9 ones?

○ 170,039

○ 1,739

○ 10,739

Which letter is inside the square and triangle, but not inside the rectangle or circle? _____

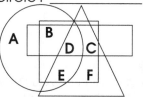

Mickey bought 3 packages of blank cassette tapes to record 17 of his favorite CDs. Each package contained 8 tapes. How many tapes did Mickey buy? _____

900
x 55

600
x 44

Day #2

Write each fraction in its simplest form.

$\frac{5}{10}$ = _____

$\frac{6}{9}$ = _____

$\frac{12}{16}$ = _____

List six multiples for

3 ____, ____, ____

____, ____, ____

4 ____, ____, ____

____, ____, ____

6 ____, ____, ____

____, ____, ____

____ is the LCM for 3, 4, and 6.

This clock shows about

○ 12:07   ○ 12:55

○ 1:00   ○ 2:10

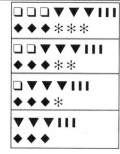

Draw the 7th box.

Day #3

Write > or < to compare.

$\frac{1}{2}$ ☐ $\frac{1}{20}$

$\frac{1}{42}$ ☐ $\frac{1}{5}$

$\frac{1}{7}$ ☐ $\frac{1}{50}$

Which is the best estimate for the length of a

fever thermometer _____

needle _____

interstate highway _____

fingernail _____

river _____

tree trunk _____

A. centimeter
B. decimeter
C. meter
D. kilometer

Write each number word.

$5\frac{3}{9}$ _____

_____

$6\frac{7}{10}$ _____

_____

$9\frac{1}{5}$ _____

_____

8)29

7)18

Day #4

S	M	T	W	Th	F	S

Fill in the dates. The third Tuesday is the 13th. Mark the 22nd and the 7th.

On what day of the week does this month begin? _____

Joe's number is greater than 25. Lil's number is a multiple of 5. Hal's number is less than Joe's. Ray's number is divisible by 8.

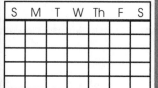

	20	23	35	40
Joe				
Lil				
Hal				
Ray				

Seventy-eight dollars was spent to buy new trees for the city park. Twelve people paid for the trees. About how much did each person spend?

○ 2 dollars

○ 6 dollars

○ 12 dollars

If these bunnies are in a magician's hat and one is drawn out, it will most likely be a _____ bunny.

Assessment

1

$$\begin{array}{r} 200 \\ \times\ 61 \\ \hline \end{array} \qquad \begin{array}{r} 400 \\ \times\ 22 \\ \hline \end{array}$$

2 $9\overline{)23}$ $6\overline{)22}$

3 ▲▲▲▲
▲❚■○

If these shapes were in a sack and you drew one out without looking, circle the shape you would most likely draw.

▲   ❚   ■   ○

4 Write each number word.

$7\frac{5}{8}$ _____

_____

$10\frac{2}{6}$ _____

_____

5 Maria was making a quilt for her 4 cousins. She used 9 material squares for each row. So far, she has sewn 6 rows. How many squares has she used? _____

6 Fill in these calendar dates.

S	M	T	W	Th	F	S

The 15th is on the third Monday. Label the 4th and the 27th. On what day of the week does this month begin? _____

7 This clock shows about

○ 6:00
○ 5:30
○ 5:33
○ 7:30

8 Which is the best estimate for the length of

a ladies handbag _____
the Hoover Dam _____
a toothpick _____
a sidewalk to the front door _____

A. centimeters   B. decimeters
C. meters   D. kilometers

9 Which number has 19 hundreds and 8 tens?

○ 1,908
○ 1,980
○ 190,008
○ 190,080

10 Ninety-one students in a youth group divided into 14 teams to go on a scavenger hunt. What is the best estimate of the number of students on each team?

○ 6
○ 16
○ 60
○ 160

Day #1

Which number shows 3 thousands, 2 hundreds, 15 tens, and 0 ones?

- ○ 30,215
- ○ 3,350
- ○ 3,215

Which figures are polygons?

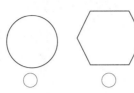

Ms. Lucas ordered 4 dozen glazed donuts and 10 chocolate donuts. Which method could be used to find the total number of donuts she ordered?

- ○ add 4 and 10
- ○ multiply 4 x 12 and add 10
- ○ subtract 4 from 10 and add 12
- ○ divide 12 by 4 and subtract 10

$$700 \times 35 \qquad 900 \times 42$$

Day #2

$$\frac{2}{6} + \frac{3}{6} = \underline{\qquad}$$

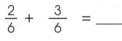

$$\frac{4}{10} + \frac{3}{10} = \underline{\qquad}$$

A. add   B. multiply

C. divide   D. subtract

_____ to find the quotient

_____ to find the sum

_____ to find the product

_____ to find the difference

Craig bought 9 folders for $0.67 each. How much money did Craig spend on folders?

_____

| ff |
| ffff |
| ffffff |
| ffffffff |

How many fs will be in the ninth box? _____

Day #3

$$\frac{1}{8} \quad \frac{1}{2} \quad \frac{1}{4} \quad \frac{1}{2} \quad \frac{1}{3}$$

Write the fractions above in order from greatest to least _____

_____

_____

_____

A. grams
B. meters
C. liters
D. centimeters
E. milliliters
F. kilograms
G. kilometers

mass _____ _____

distance _____

_____ _____

volume _____ _____

Which number line shows the whole numbers that are greater than 43 and less than 49? _____

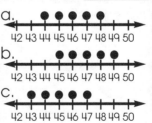

a.
42 43 44 45 46 47 48 49 50

b.
42 43 44 45 46 47 48 49 50

c.
42 43 44 45 46 47 48 49 50

★★★★★★★★
★★★★★★★★
★★★★
$$8\overline{)20}$$

★★★★★
★★★★★
★★★★★
★★★★★
★★★★★
$$9\overline{)25}$$

Day #4

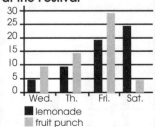

Refreshments Sold at the Festival

30
25
20
15
10
5
0
   Wed.   Th.   Fri.   Sat.

■ lemonade
▨ fruit punch

On which day was more lemonade than fruit punch sold? _____

Joey lives 10 blocks to the east of Ned. Ned lives 2 blocks to the east of Sue. Fran lives 7 blocks to the east of Sue. How many blocks is it from Fran's to Joey's house? _____

How many blocks is it from Fran's to Ned's house? _____

Twenty-one thousand, eight hundred ninety-nine people attended a football game. It began raining and 2,688 people left. About how many people remained at the game?

- ○ 10,000
- ○ 19,000
- ○ 20,000
- ○ 23,000

A ■■□□□□

B ■■□□□□□□

If these tiles are placed in a box and one is drawn out, which box, A or B, would give the best chance of drawing a black tile?

_____

Assessment

1

$$400 \times 83$$ $$200 \times 79$$

2

$$5\overline{)34}$$ $$7\overline{)53}$$

3 Thirty-three thousand, five hundred eighty-nine people booked flights in December. Five thousand, one hundred two people canceled their flights because of snowstorms. About how many people kept their flights?

○ 28,000   ○ 30,000

○ 38,000   ○ 20,000

4 For a bake sale, Ms. Murphy baked 7 dozen cookies and 5 cakes. Which method could be used to find the number of baked goods Ms. Murphy prepared?

○ add 7 and 5

○ divide 12 by 5 and add 7

○ subtract 5 from 84

○ multiply 7 by 12 and add 5

5 Match.

A. multiplication   _____ sum

B. division   _____ difference

C. addition   _____ product

D. subtraction   _____ quotient

6

$$\frac{1}{10} \quad \frac{1}{8} \quad \frac{1}{25} \quad \frac{1}{3} \quad \frac{1}{16}$$

Write these fractions in order from least to greatest.

_____, _____, _____, _____, _____

7 Which number shows 6 thousands, 7 hundreds, 12 tens, and 9 ones?

○ 67,129

○ 6,829

○ 6,709

○ 76,129

8 Which figures are polygons?

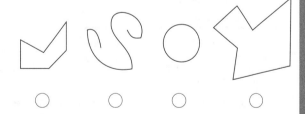

○   ○   ○   ○

9 Lynn sold 8 games at her garage sale. She charged $0.95 for each game. How much money did she make by selling her games at the garage sale?_____

10 The graph shows the points made by the boys' team and the girls' team in a volleyball tournament. In which game did the boys and the girls score the same number of points? _____

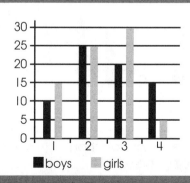

Which number shows 22 thousands, 13 hundreds, and 9 ones?

○ 22,139

○ 22,309

○ 23,309

How many faces does this figure have? _____

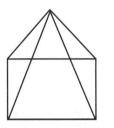

Jamie had 25 sand art packages. She gave 10 to her little sister. Then she bought 8 more. Which equation could be used to find the number of sand art packages Jamie has now?

○ (25 + 10) + 8

○ (25 + 10) − 8

○ (25 − 10) + 8

852
x   5

437
x   6

Subtract.

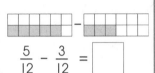

$\frac{5}{12} - \frac{3}{12} =$ ☐

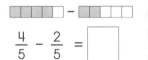

$\frac{4}{5} - \frac{2}{5} =$ ☐

Underline the true equations.

(4 x 5) + 3 = 4 x (5 + 3)

(5 x 2) x 2 = 5 x (2 x 2)

(9 x 1) − 1 = 9 x (1 − 1)

(4 x 4) ÷ 1 = 4 x (4 ÷ 1)

Carlos practices his clarinet for one half-hour each day. What is the total number of hours Carlos practices in five days? _____

How many Vs will be in the 20th box? _____

vvvvv

vvvvv
vvvvv

vvvvv
vvvvv
vvvvv

vvvvv
vvvvv
vvvvv
vvvvv

$\frac{2}{15}$ $\frac{2}{12}$ $\frac{2}{9}$ $\frac{2}{42}$ $\frac{2}{5}$

Write the above fractions in order from greatest to least. _____

_____

_____

_____

_____

Circle the best unit for measuring

1. the distance across Africa

centimeters   meters
decimeters   kilometers

2. the height of a swing set

centimeters   meters
decimeters   kilometers

Write each number using numerals.

four-fifths   _____

two-thirds   _____

seven-eights   _____

Solve.

7)54

6)23

Pounds of Recyclables Collected

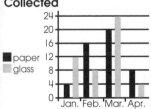

■ paper
▨ glass

Comparing totals, the pounds of paper recycled is (>, <, =) to the pounds of recycled glass.

These are klinkers.

These are NOT klinkers.

Which of these are klinkers?

There are 1,460 paintings and 3,977 drawings entered in a children's art festival. There were also 315 collages and 89 clay sculptures entered. About how many total entries were there?

○ between 5,000 and 6,000

○ between 6,000 and 7,000

○ between 4,000 and 5,000

 A   B

The chances of drawing a ☐ are

○ greater with box A

○ greater with box B

○ equal with box A or B

Name _____

Assessment

1

$$436 \times 4 \qquad 925 \times 9$$

2

$8\overline{)77} \qquad 6\overline{)53}$

3

A | w w w a a a a a

B | w w w a a a

The chances of drawing a w are (greater, less, or equal) with box B. _____

---

4 Write each fraction using numerals.

seven-ninths _____

four-fifths _____

one-third _____

---

5 Michael had 72 baseball cards. He traded 20 to his friend for a yo-yo. The next week, Michael got 13 more baseball cards for his birthday. Which equation could be used to find out how many baseball cards Michael has now?

○ (72 − 20) + 13   ○ (72 + 20) + 13

○ 72 − (20 − 13)   ○ 72 + 13

---

6 1. The total number of votes for football was (>, <, =) the votes for soccer.

2. Which grades had the same number of votes for soccer?

_____ and _____

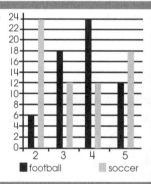

■ football   ▨ soccer

---

7 It takes Maria 15 minutes to walk home from school each day. In 2 weeks, how many hours does she spend walking home from school?

_____

---

8 Circle the best unit for measuring.

1. The height of a house

centimeters   decimeters

meters   kilometers

2. the distance of a trolley ride around town

centimeters   decimeters

meters   kilometers

---

9 Which number shows 34 thousands, 17 hundreds, and 6 tens?

○ 34,176

○ 35,760

○ 37,460

○ 34,706

---

10 In a statewide science fair, there were 2,398 projects exhibited on recycling and 1,598 projects on solar energy. The fair also had 79 ecology projects and 221 electricity projects. About how many projects were exhibited at the science fair?

○ between 2,000 and 3,000

○ between 3,000 and 4,000

○ between 4,000 and 5,000

○ between 5,000 and 6,000

Which number shows 10 thousands, 22 hundreds, and 4 tens?

○ 12,240

○ 20,224

○ 22,104

How many faces does this figure have? _____

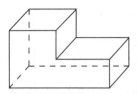

Xavier shared a package of 37 pizza bites with 4 of his friends. If all the boys ate the same number of pizza bites, how many were left over?

_____

$$705$$
$$\times \quad 6$$

$$\frac{5}{9} + \frac{2}{9} = \_\_\_$$

$$\frac{3}{12} + \frac{7}{12} = \_\_\_$$

Write each fraction as a whole number or mixed number in its simplest form.

$$\frac{24}{3} \quad \_\_\_\_\_$$

$$\frac{30}{7} \quad \_\_\_\_\_$$

Underline the true equations.

$(9 + 8) + 7 = 9 + (8 + 7)$

$(8 \times 4) \times 0 = 8 \times (4 \times 0)$

$(12 - 3) - 2 = 12 - (3 - 2)$

$(6 \times 6) \div 1 = 6 \times (6 \div 1)$

Computer Lab Minutes Used per Week

Grade	M	T	W	Th	F
3	15		15		
4		30		45	
5	15		60		15

For the week shown, how many minutes was the computer lab used?

_____ minutes =

_____ hours _____ minutes

| 384 |
| 192 |
| 96 |
| 48 |

What number will be in the 7th box?

[ ]

$$\frac{30}{3} \quad \frac{4}{2} \quad \frac{16}{2} \quad \frac{20}{5}$$

Write the fractions in order from least to greatest.

_____

_____

_____

_____

What is the area of the figure shown on the grid?

_____ square units

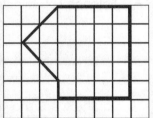

Write each mixed number using numerals.

six and seven-tenths

_____

ten and four-fifths

_____

fifteen and eight-twentieths

_____

$4\overline{)84}$

$$\frac{7}{16} - \frac{4}{16} = \_\_\_$$

$$\frac{4}{5} - \frac{3}{5} = \_\_\_$$

Temperatures for the School Week

The greatest difference in temperature occurred between which two days? _____ and _____

These are gloopies.

These are NOT gloopies

Which of these are gloopies?

Two thousand, three hundred seventy-eight people came on the opening day of the county fair. One thousand nine hundred thirty-two people came the next day. On the third day, 781 people came, and on the last day, 1,032 people came. About how many people came to the fair?

○ between 4,000 and 5,000

○ between 5,000 and 6,000

○ between 6,000 and 7,000

▲▲▲
✚✚✚

The chances of drawing a ▲ are

○ greater than drawing a ✚

○ less than drawing a ✚

○ equal to drawing a ✚

Assessment

1

$$903 \times 7 \qquad 201 \times 8$$

2

$$4\overline{)88} \qquad 2\overline{)64}$$

3 Seven thousand eight hundred two visitors attended the museum's African exhibit. Two thousand, one hundred seven visitors attended the Egyptian exhibit, and 5,890 visitors saw the Japanese exhibit. About how many visitors attended these exhibits?

- ○ between 14,000 and 15,000
- ○ between 15,000 and 16,000
- ○ between 16,000 and 17,000

4 Natasha bought a package of cookies to share with her 6 friends. The package contained 45 cookies. If Natasha and her friends each get the same number of cookies, how many cookies will be leftover? _____

5 Which equations are true?

- ○ $(12 + 5) - 4 = 12 + (5 - 4)$
- ○ $(6 \times 5) \times 0 = 6 \times (5 \times 0)$
- ○ $(9 \times 8) \div 1 = 9 \times (8 \div 1)$
- ○ $(14 - 5) - 2 = 14 - (5 - 2)$

6

$$\frac{25}{5} \quad \frac{21}{7} \quad \frac{30}{5} \quad \frac{18}{9} \quad \frac{54}{6}$$

Write the above fractions in order from greatest to least.

_____ _____ _____ _____ _____

7 Which number shows 50 thousands, 35 hundreds, and 4 tens?

- ○ 50,354
- ○ 55,304
- ○ 53,540
- ○ 5,354

8 How many faces does this figure have? _____

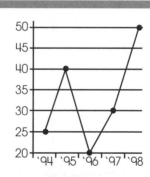

9 **Science Lab Minutes Used per Week**

Grade	M	T	W	Th	F
2	30		30		30
3	45			45	
4	20	20	20		30

For the week shown on the chart, how many minutes was the science lab in use?

_____ minutes = _____ hours _____ minutes

10 The graph shows the average temperature for the month of February during the years 1994–1998. During which two years was the difference in the average temperature the greatest?
_____ and _____   _____ and _____

During which two years was it the least?
_____ and _____

       0-7682-3205-8 *Math 4 Today*

Chama flipped through the dictionary. The page he landed on had a 4 in the ones place, a 5 in the thousands place, and a 2 in the tens place. What was Chama's page number? _____

How many corners does this figure have? _____

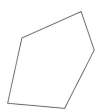

Mrs. Hernandez made coffee for the 7 members of her bridge club. Her coffee maker makes 30 cups. If she and her club members drink an equal number of cups, how many cups of coffee will still be in the coffee maker when her guests leave? _____

$$\begin{array}{r} 22 \\ \times\ 13 \end{array} \Big\} \quad \begin{array}{r} 20 + 2 \\ \times\ \quad 3 \end{array}$$

$$\begin{array}{r} 34 \\ \times\ 32 \end{array} \quad \begin{array}{r} 20 + 2 \\ \times\ \quad 10 \end{array}$$

Write each fraction as a whole number or mixed number in its simplest form.

$\frac{31}{3}$ = _____

$\frac{45}{7}$ = _____

Which equation does NOT belong?

○ 7 x 8 = 56

○ 8 x 7 = 56

○ 56 ÷ 8 = 7

○ 7 + 8 = 15

What time will the clock show in 2 hours and 45 minutes? _____

9
18
27
36

What number will be in the 10th box?

▢

Write >, <, or = to compare.

$\frac{4}{2}$ ▢ $1\frac{1}{5}$

$2\frac{3}{8}$ ▢ $\frac{20}{4}$

$5\frac{2}{8}$ ▢ $\frac{42}{8}$

What is the area of the figure shown on the grid?

_____ square units

What is the approximate perimeter?

_____ units

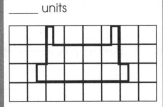

Which mixed number belongs where you see the letter A?

○ $15\frac{1}{32}$

○ $15\frac{1}{2}$

○ $15\frac{7}{8}$

$7\overline{)490}$

$9\overline{)1,800}$

Plant Growth after 3 Weeks

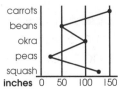

Circle the best estimate of the growth difference between the squash and peas.

100 in.   150 in.   50 in.

Use the graph to the left. Together the peas and the _____ grew about the same as the squash.

Shade the chart below that matches the graph.

carrots	150	carrots	150
beans	50	beans	50
okra	100	okra	100
peas	25	peas	50
squash	125	squash	100

Three thousand, five hundred ninety-three people were seated in 9 rows of stadium bleachers. About how many people were sitting in each row?

○ 200

○ 300

○ 400

○ 500

Tymo wants to mount his 6 miniature puzzles in one frame. What information does Tymo need before buying the frame?

○ the number of pieces in each puzzle

○ the combined areas of the puzzles

○ the cost of the puzzles

Assessment

1

$$31 \times 12 \qquad 13 \times 23$$

2

$$6\overline{)360} \qquad 8\overline{)5,600}$$

3

| 12 |
| 24 |
| 36 |
| 48 |

What number will be in the 8th box? [ ]

4

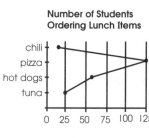

A

24 25 26 27 28 29 30

Which mixed number belongs where you see the letter A?

○ $26\frac{1}{2}$ ○ $27\frac{1}{8}$ ○ $27\frac{11}{12}$ ○ $27\frac{1}{2}$

5 Jeff's mother made pizzas for his birthday. She sliced the pizzas into 50 slices. She served Jeff and his 7 guests the same number of slices, and she ate the rest. How many pieces of pizza did Jeff's mother eat? _____

6

Number of Students Ordering Lunch Items

chili
pizza
hot dogs
tuna

0 25 50 75 100 125

Complete the chart.

Item	Number Ordered
tuna	_____
_____	15
_____	55
pizza	_____

7 What time will the clock show in 4 hours and 15 minutes? _____

8 What is the area of the figure shown on the grid? _____ square units

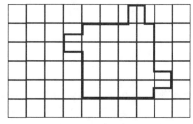

9 Heather wrote a number with a 6 in the ones place, a 2 in the thousands place, and a 9 in the tens place. What number did Heather write?

_____

10 Five thousand, five hundred twenty-one illustrations are included in a 6 volume set of children's dictionaries. About how many illustrations are in each volume?

○ 600

○ 700

○ 800

○ 900

Day #1

Leslie was writing the populations of several cities. The population of Nawton has a 9 in the thousands place, a 5 in the ones place, and a 6 in the ten thousands place. What number did Leslie write for Nawton's population? _____

How many corners does this figure have? _____

Adam is studying for an end-of-semester spelling test. There are 6 word lists that have 15 words each. Adam studies for his spelling test by writing the words 3 times. How many words will Adam write? _____

$$\begin{array}{r} 45 \\ \times\ 25 \end{array} \Big\}$$ $$\begin{array}{r} 40+5 \\ \times\qquad 5 \end{array}$$

$$\begin{array}{r} 62 \\ \times\ 43 \end{array}$$ $$\begin{array}{r} 40+5 \\ \times\qquad 20 \end{array}$$

Day #2

Add or subtract. Simplify if needed.

$\dfrac{5}{8} + \dfrac{2}{8} =$ _____

$\dfrac{2}{10} + \dfrac{1}{10} =$ _____

$\dfrac{4}{6} - \dfrac{2}{6} =$ _____

To find the average of a group of numbers, add the numbers together. Then divide the total by the number of addends.

Find the average for

8, 7, 2, 3, 15

_____

Robert saved $52.00 so he could attend a concert. He paid $23.50 for the tickets. At the concert, he bought a program for $7.25 and a T-shirt for $15.00. How much money did Robert have after the concert? _____

88, 81, 74, 67, 60

What is the rule for the pattern?

_____

Day #3

Write >, <, or = to compare.

$\dfrac{9}{3}$ ☐ $3\dfrac{1}{3}$

$7\dfrac{1}{4}$ ☐ $\dfrac{30}{4}$

$2\dfrac{1}{16}$ ☐ $\dfrac{20}{4}$

Write >, <, or = to compare.

3 inches ☐ 3 yards

6 feet ☐ 2 yards

12 inches ☐ 1 foot

8 feet ☐ 1 yard

Which mixed number belongs where you see the letter A?

12 —|—|—|—A—|— 13

○ $13\dfrac{1}{2}$

○ $12\dfrac{1}{2}$

○ $12\dfrac{3}{4}$

$3\overline{)9,360}$

$4\overline{)8,048}$

Day #4

James ☙☙☙☙☙☙
Kevin ☙☙☙☙☙☙
Steve ☙☙☙☙☙☙

each ☙ = 8

Shade in the trees on the graph to show that Kevin trimmed 36 trees. Steve trimmed 44 trees. James trimmed 20 trees.

Use the graph to the left. How many trees were trimmed by all the boys? _____

One-half a tree shaded = _____ trees

Steve trimmed about _____ times the number of trees trimmed by James.

One thousand, five hundred ninety-three people were waiting to board 8 planes. About how many passengers will get on each plane?

○ 100

○ 200

○ 300

○ 400

Mrs. Jordan needs to make lemonade for the school's field day. A can of lemonade serves 30 people. What information does Mrs. Jordan need before she makes the lemonade?

○ the cost of the lemonade per can

○ how many cans it takes to make a gallon

○ the number of people who will drink lemonade

Assessment

1

$$67 \times 26$$ $$39 \times 47$$

2

$7\overline{)4,200}$ $8\overline{)5,600}$

3 During 1 week, 5,598 people booked tours. The tour line has 7 buses. About how many people did each bus carry during the week?

○ 600   ○ 700

○ 800   ○ 900

4 During 25 days at summer camp, Lisbet swam 3 times a day. She swam 20 meters each time. How many meters did Lisbet swim during summer camp? _____

5 Find the average for this group of numbers.

17, 3, 12, 8, 5 _____

6 Write >, <, or = to compare.

4   □ $\frac{12}{3}$

$2\frac{4}{5}$ □ $2\frac{6}{5}$

$5\frac{7}{3}$ □ $7\frac{1}{3}$

7 Weston used his computer's word count on a report he was writing. The computer counted the words in his report and displayed a 9 in the hundreds place. How many words were in Weston's report? _____

8 How many corners does the figure have? _____

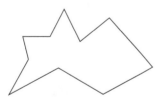

9 Javier saved $72.30 to buy some new computer games. He bought Rocket Race for $22.77 and Pro Ball for $19.85. The tax on the two CDs was $5.75. How much did Javier have after buying the games? _____

10 Add or subtract. Write the answer in simplest form.

$\frac{3}{7} + \frac{1}{7} = $ ___ $\frac{6}{16} - \frac{2}{16} = $ ___ $\frac{7}{9} - \frac{5}{9} = $ ___

Day #1

30,000 + 7,000 + 200 + 3 =

- ○ 37,230
- ○ 372,003
- ○ 30,702,003
- ○ 37,203

Write C if the figures are congruent. Write S if they are similar.

____

____

____

Neva bought 3 packages of gum. Each package has 12 pieces. How can Neva share the gum with 8 of her friends so that she and her friends each get the same number of pieces?

_____

$$\begin{array}{r} 15 \\ \times\ 75 \\ \hline \end{array}$$

$$\begin{array}{r} 6,247 \\ +\ 4,788 \\ \hline \end{array}$$

Day #2

Add or subtract. Simplify.

$\frac{5}{12} + \frac{4}{12} =$ ____

$\frac{8}{13} - \frac{5}{13} =$ ____

$\frac{12}{32} + \frac{12}{32} =$ ____

The range of a group of numbers is the difference between the least and the greatest number in the group. The median of a group of numbers is the middle number when the group is arranged from least to greatest.

8, 5, 3, 20, and 2

the range = ____

the median = ____

Janette bought nail polish for $3.89, 2 tubes of lip gloss for $2.49 each, and perfume for $9.22. The total after tax was added was $19.54. How much tax did Janette pay on the items she bought?

_____

2, 9, 23, 51, 107

What is the rule for the pattern?

_____

_____

Day #3

Some of the Largest Earth-Filled Dams Measured in Cubic Yards

Tarbela	186,000,000
Oahe	92,000,000
Cornelia	274,026,000
Pati	261,590
Atatürk	110,522

List the names of the dams in order of size from least to greatest. _____

____ ____

____ ____

Write >, <, or = to compare.

24 inches ▢ 3 feet

9 feet ▢ 3 yards

36 inches ▢ 1 yard

10 feet ▢ 2 yards

Which number is read two hundred seventy-five million, nine hundred thousand, forty-six?

- ○ 275,900,046
- ○ 275,946
- ○ 200,759,460

$5\overline{)4,525}$

$9\overline{)7,245}$

Day #4

Margie's Gift Wrapping

Sept.	▪▪▪▪▪▮
Oct.	▪▪▪
Nov.	▪▪▪▪▪▪▪
Dec.	▪▪▪▪▪▪▪▪

each ▪ = 50 gifts wrapped

How many gifts were wrapped in October? _____

How many gifts were wrapped in September? _____

Use the graph to the left. How many gifts were wrapped during all four months? _____

How many more gifts were wrapped in November and December than were wrapped in September? _____

How many more ▪ would be needed to show 250 gifts wrapped in October? _____

What is 675,789 rounded to the nearest thousand?

- ○ 700,000
- ○ 676,000
- ○ 680,000
- ○ 674,000

Shane spent $25.00 on vacation souvenirs. His mother spent $40.00, and his dad spent $30.00. Judy, Shane's sister, spent more than Shane and Dad but less than Mother. Which could be true?

- ○ Judy spent $45.00.
- ○ Judy spent $32.00.
- ○ Judy spent $29.00.

Assessment

1

$$\begin{array}{r} 69 \\ \times 47 \\ \hline \end{array} \qquad \begin{array}{r} 3,987 \\ + 4,776 \\ \hline \end{array}$$

2

$$4\overline{)3,624} \qquad 3\overline{)1,512}$$

3 6, 21, 66, 201

What is the rule for the above pattern?

_____

_____

4 **Match.**

1. three hundred ninety-five million, two hundred six thousand, four hundred one _____

2. three million, ninety-five thousand, two hundred sixty-one _____

3. thirty-nine thousand, two hundred sixty-four _____

A. 395,206,401   B. 39,264   C. 3,095,261

5 Ron bought 3 boxes of juice drinks for his track team. Each box contains 6 drinks. If Ron and his 8 team members each have the same number of juice drinks, how many will each person receive? _____

6 **Operator Assisted Phone Calls from Hotel Farrington**

May	☎ ☎ ☎ ☎
June	☎ ☎ ☎ ☎ ☎
July	☎ ☎ ☎ ☎ ☎ ☎ ☎
Aug.	☎ ☎ ☎ ☎ ☎ ☎

Each ☎ = 80

How many calls were made in June? _____
How many calls were made in August? _____
How many more calls were made in August than in May? _____
In all, how many calls were made? _____

7 Emil earned $57.00 doing odd jobs. Mark earned more than Emil, but less than Jake. Jake earned $72.00. Which could be true?

○ Mark earned $55.00.

○ Mark earned $75.00.

○ Mark earned $67.00.

8 Write >, < or = to compare.

36 inches	☐	2 feet
3 yards	☐	9 feet
24 inches	☐	1 foot
1 yard	☐	24 inches

9

$60,000 + 3,000 + 500 + 4 =$ _____

$500,000 + 80,000 + 2,000 + 1 =$ _____

$20,000 + 300 + 90 + 7 =$ _____

10 What is 782,432 rounded to the nearest thousand?

○ 780,000

○ 790,000

○ 781,400

○ 782,000

What is 816,120 rounded to the nearest thousand?

○ 810,000

○ 816,000

○ 822,400

○ 825,000

Day #1

500,000 + 30,000 + 400 + 20 + 7 =

○ 530,427

○ 500,003,427

○ 53,427

○ 534,270

Write C if the figures are congruent. Write S if they are similar.

____

____

____

Mrs. Baker picked 22 red flowers, 40 yellow flowers, 58 miniature daisies, and 24 white flower buds from her garden. She placed the same number of plants in each of 4 baskets. How many plants are in each basket? _____

$$315 \times 7$$

$$7,938 + 2,677$$

Day #2

Add or subtract the fractions. Simplify.

$9 \frac{5}{7} - 4 \frac{4}{7} =$ _____

$3 \frac{1}{12} + 7 \frac{5}{12} =$ _____

$16 \frac{8}{24} - 5 \frac{5}{24} =$ _____

Find the median, range, and mean for the following group of numbers.

13, 57, 23, 42, 15

median = _____

range = _____

mean = _____

What time will the clock show in 2 hours and 25 minutes? _____

| 1, 1 | 2, 4 | 3, 9 |

| 4, 16 | 5, 25 |

What would the 8th box look like?

Day #3

**Some Famous Volcanoes
Height in Feet**

Aconcagua	22,831
Lassen	10,457
Mauna Loa	13,677
Cotopaxi	19,347
Mt. Etna	11,122

List the names of the volcanoes in order of height from greatest to least.

_____, _____,

_____, _____,

_____

The temperature on this thermometer shows about _____ degrees Celsius.

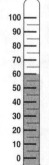

Which number is read three million, nine hundred sixty-two thousand, four hundred twenty-one?

○ 396,241

○ 3,962,421

○ 300,962,421

$$8,247 - 5,872$$

$$5,104 - 2,652$$

Day #4

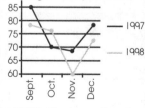

In 1997, the month of _____ had about the same temperature as the month of _____ in 1998.

| 2 | 12 | 5 | 7 |
| 9 | 11 | 3 | 6 |

If 3 bean bags were tossed onto the above board so that no number was repeated, what could be a possible score?

○ 50   ○ 8

○ 32   ○ 100

Round these numbers to the nearest ten thousand.

775,320 _____

621,990 _____

482,589 _____

907,125 _____

Using only the above beads, what is a possible arrangement?

○

○

○

Assessment

1

$$209 \times 8 \qquad 8,356 + 3,784$$

2

$$6,159 - 4,882$$

3 Round these numbers to the nearest ten thousand.

884,298 _____

466,132 _____

525,017 _____

4 Andy bought 55 gumdrops, 82 peppermints, 50 sour balls, and 35 lemon drops to fill 6 candy jars for the nursing home. How many pieces of candy will he put in each jar?

_____

5 Find the median, range, and mean for this group of numbers.

13, 12, 5, 26, 11, 8, 9

median _____

range _____

mean _____

6 List the months in order from greatest to least amount of water used for lawn care.

_____

_____

_____

_____

Gallons of Water Used for Lawn Care in Reskin, Illinois	
May	89,129
June	92,456
July	89,752
August	92,488

7 $900,000 + 80,000 + 2,000 + 400 + 80 =$

_____

$70,000 + 1,000 + 50 + 1 =$

_____

$200,000 + 3,000 + 600 + 70 + 8 =$

_____

8 Write C if the figures are congruent. Write S if they are similar.

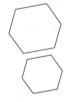 

_____   _____   _____

9 What time will the clock show in 2 hours and 35 minutes? _____

10 Bowling Scores

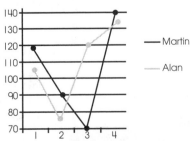

During which game did Alan and Martin score about the same? _____

During which game was the difference in their scores the greatest? _____

Write in expanded form.

43,209

_____

_____

_____

_____

Label S for slide and F for flip.

____

____

____

____

Angie had 408 stickers on 8 pages of her sticker album. If each page has the same number of stickers, which equation could be used to show the number of stickers on each page?

○ 408 + 8 = 416

○ 408 − 8 = 400

○ 408 x 8 = 3,264

○ 408 ÷ 8 = 51

```
   942
 x   8
```

```
 9,527
+4,658
```

Day #1

Simplify.

$3\frac{16}{12}$ = ____

$9\frac{24}{8}$ = ____

$7\frac{32}{6}$ = ____

Find the median, range, and mean for this group of numbers.

2, 16, 32, 15, 3, 9, 7

median = _____

range = _____

mean = _____

Tristan arrives at school at 8:15. He has 4 hours and 20 minutes of classes until lunch time. At what time does Tristan eat lunch?

_____

| 1, 4 | 2, 5 | 3, 6 |

| 4, 7 | 5, 8 |

What would the 21st box look like?

[ ]

Day #2

Which group of numbers is in order from greatest to least?

○ 7,234; 7,432; 7,243

○ 8,021; 8,012; 8,003

○ 5,921; 5,812; 5,993

○ 2,005; 2,415; 2,501

Shade in this thermometer to show about 75 degrees Celsius.

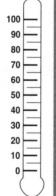

300 305 310 315 320

This number line shows

○ multiples of 5 between 305 and 345

○ multiples of 10 between 300 and 330

○ multiples of 5 between 295 and 325

```
 5,040
-3,217
```

```
 9,200
-7,643
```

Day #3

Money Earned Doing Odd Jobs

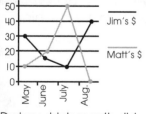

During which month did Jim and Matt earn about the same amount of money? _____

If 3 darts burst 3 of the above balloons, what could be a possible score?

○ 50

○ 45

○ 15

○ 38

A reasonable estimate of the number of hours a fourth-grade student might spend doing homework during the week would be about

○ 100 hours

○ 45 hours

○ 5 hours

○ 1 hour

Mighty Marvels Video Game

Player	Score
Jason	2,450
Roger	3,100
Alex	4,200

The answer is 1,750. Using the chart, write a question for this answer. _____
_____
_____

Day #4

Name _____

Assessment

1

$$934 \times 7$$

$$6,107 + 7,999$$

2

$$8,020 - 2,731$$

3

| 10, 9 | 20, 19 |
| 30, 29 | 40, 39 |

What would the 12th box look like? ☐

4

196 200 204 208 212 216 220 224 228

This number line shows

○ multiples of 2 between 194 and 230

○ multiples of 4 between 192 and 232

○ multiples of 5 between 195 and 230

5 Kyle has 105 models on 5 shelves. If each shelf has the same number of models, which equation could be used to find the number of models on each shelf?

○ $105 \div 5 = 21$ ○ $105 \times 5 = 525$

○ $105 - 5 = 100$ ○ $105 + 5 = 110$

6

Pages Read by Kay and Gina

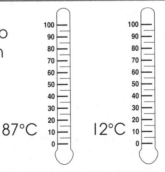

— Kay   — Gina

On which day was the difference in pages read the greatest? _____

On which day was the difference in pages read the least? _____

On which day did both girls read more than 35 pages? _____

7 Summer school classes begin at 8:45 and last for 4 and a $\frac{1}{2}$ hours. At what time do summer school classes end? _____

8 Shade in each thermometer to show the given temperature.

87°C   12°C

9 Write the expanded form.

27,170 _____

_____

50,936 _____

_____

10 A reasonable estimate of the number of hours a student might spend watching television during the school week would be about

○ 1 hour

○ 10 hours

○ 100 hours

○ 1,000 hours

Write in expanded form. 390,682

_____

_____

_____

_____

_____

Label S for slide and F for flip.

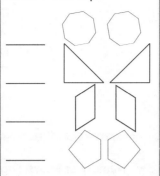

____

____

____

____

Luis is reading a novel for a book report due on Friday. His novel has 150 pages. He read 27 pages on Monday, 42 pages on Tuesday, and 59 pages on Wednesday. How many more pages must he read to finish the book? _____

42
x 20

93
x 30

Add and simplify.

$2\frac{1}{3} + 8\frac{2}{3} =$ _____

$4\frac{3}{12} + 7\frac{10}{12} =$ _____

$9\frac{1}{4} + 5\frac{3}{4} =$ _____

Bowling League Finals

Team	Points Scored
A	767
B	906
C	760
D	851
E	593

Which teams scored an odd number of points? _____

Sheila saw these ads in the newspaper.

Maxi's Essentials	Sav-Co
$19.95	$21.98
$2.98	$15.25
$25.00	$2.50

How much money can Sheila save by buying the three items at Sav-Co? _____

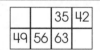

		35	42
49	56	63	

What numbers go in the three empty boxes? _____

_____

_____

Which group of numbers is in order from least to greatest?

○ 6,434; 6,532; 6,943

○ 5,021; 5,012; 5,003

○ 9,921; 8,812; 8,983

○ 1,005; 1,015; 1,001

The keys weigh

grams

○ 1 gram

○ more than 1 gram

○ less than 1 gram

○ 100 grams

0 6 12 18 24 30 36

This number line shows

○ 24 − 6 = 19

○ 24 ÷ 2 = 12

○ 6 × 4 = 24

○ 6 + 6 + 6 + 6 = 24

9,010
− 8,736

$6\overline{)636}$

Bicycle Color Choices

red

blue

pink

black

⬛ = 20 votes

Circle the true statements.

A. The number of people who chose red was twice the number who chose blue.

B. Blue received the fewest votes.

Use the graph to the left.

C. Pink received 60 votes.

D. Black received 20 less votes than red.

E. Blue received 100 votes.

F. The difference between the number of votes received by black and blue is 60.

G. The number of votes received by pink is one-half those received by black.

If you use 1 sheet of notebook paper for each of 4 different subjects every day, about how many sheets of notebook paper will you use in 2 weeks?

○ 200 sheets

○ 100 sheets

○ 40 sheets

○ 5 sheets

Greg ate 3 slices of pizza. Joey ate 3 times as many as Greg, but 4 less than Mark. Mario ate 2 more slices than Greg. On the back of this paper, write a question for each answer given below.

A. 5 slices

B. 13 slices

C. 30 slices

Assessment

1

$$\begin{array}{r} 64 \\ \times\ 20 \\ \hline \end{array} \qquad \begin{array}{r} 4{,}070 \\ -\ 2{,}398 \\ \hline \end{array}$$

2

$$8\overline{)648}$$

3 Billy reads an average of 7 pages a night during the school week. About how many pages will he read in 3 weeks?

○ 35   ○ 50
○ 100   ○ 135

4 Jay's baseball team set a goal of getting 5 more runs this season than in the last 3 seasons combined. In 2002, the team had 23 runs, in 2003 the team had 19 runs, and in 2004, they had 14 runs. So far this year, they have 17 runs. How many more runs does Jay's team need in order to meet their goal? _____

5

Number of Babysitting Jobs Last Year	
Milly	72
Jean	24
Susan	63
Andrea	41
Carla	58

Which girls had an even number of babysitting jobs last year?

_____

_____

6 Which group of numbers is in order from least to greatest?

○ 7,892; 7,880; 7,782

○ 5,208; 5,590; 5,579

○ 6,890; 6,895; 6,080

○ 3,207; 3,227; 3,303

7 Write the expanded form.

801,267 _____

_____

420,198 _____

_____

8 Label S for slide and F for flip.

___   ___

___   ___

9 Mrs. Amyx usually buys burgers at Dot's Drive-In, but this week Busy B's is having a sale. How much will Mrs. Amyx save by buying 4 burgers, 4 fries, and 4 shakes at Busy B's? _____

Dot's Drive-In		Busy B's	
4 burgers	$14.45	4 burgers	$12.25
4 fries	$8.75	4 fries	$7.50
4 shakes	$8.80	4 shakes	$8.00

10 Add or subtract. Simplify the fractions.

$$15\frac{3}{7} - 7\frac{5}{7} = \underline{\quad} \qquad 6\frac{9}{18} + 8\frac{11}{18} = \underline{\quad} \qquad 5\frac{5}{20} + 9\frac{15}{20} = \underline{\quad}$$

Which number shows 7 hundred thousands, 12 ten thousands, 4 hundreds, and 2 tens?

- ○ 701,242
- ○ 712,420
- ○ 820,420
- ○ 802,452

Name the vertex of each angle.

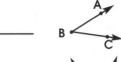

_____

_____

_____

Before dieting, Debra weighed 132 pounds. She lost an average of 2 pounds a month last year. Which equation shows how to find Debra's current weight?

- ○ 132 – 2 = 130
- ○ 132 – (2 x 12) = 108
- ○ 132 ÷ (2 x 6) = 11

267
x 300

578
x 600

Day #1

Write the fraction and the decimal shown by each model.

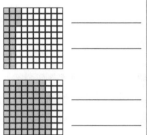

_____

_____

_____

Which number could be a remainder when dividing by 6?
- ○ 4
- ○ 7
- ○ 9

Which number could be a remainder when dividing by 10?
- ○ 15
- ○ 25
- ○ 8

Ms. Wan needs 2 pounds of coffee, 6 pounds of sugar, and 20 paper plates. Which store will save her money on these items? _____

Food Town

1 pound coffee	$3.50
2 pound bag sugar	$2.00
10 pack paper plates	$2.25

Mini Market

2 pounds coffee	$7.50
3 pound bag sugar	$2.50
5 pack paper plates	$1.00

63	69	75	81	57

What numbers go in the three empty boxes? _____

_____

_____

Day #2

Dictionary	Number of Entry Words
Maridim's	467,897
Collegiate	674,987
Duke Press	460,809
Gorktles	669,989

List the dictionaries in order from the least number of entry words to the greatest number.

_____

_____

_____

The paper fan weighs

- ○ 3 grams
- ○ more than 9 grams
- ○ less than 9 grams
- ○ 9 grams

Write the number words.

45,206 _____

_____

_____

631,520 _____

_____

2,000
– 1,218

4)929

Day #3

Garden	Flowers Blooming
Mrs. Willis	24
Ms. Jones	36
Mr. Bates	44
Miss Sax	52

Draw a picture graph on the back of this paper that shows the chart data above.

each ❀ = 8

Mystery Numbers

A = C ÷ 7
B = a multiple of 5 less than 20
C = B + 6
D = A x C

A = _____

B = _____

C = _____

D = _____

Round each number to the nearest 10.

467,125 _____

235,942 _____

551,932 _____

248,701 _____

A

B

The chances of drawing a ◆ are

- ○ equal between box A and B
- ○ 3 times greater with box B
- ○ 2 times greater with box B

Day #4

1

398   5,000
x 600   x 4,231

2

5)288

3

			65
74	83	92	101

What numbers go in the three empty boxes?

_____, _____, _____

4 Write the number words.

503,291 _____

_____

48,603 _____

_____

5 Eight months ago Tad weighed 98 pounds. He has gained an average of 3 pounds a month. Which equation could be used to find Tad's current weight?

○ 98 – 8 =   ○ 98 – (3 x 8)

○ 98 x 3 =   ○ 98 + (3 x 8)

6

Snow Cones Sold

Blueberry Ice	33	Coconut Freeze	27
Mocha Cream	18	Cherry Blizzard	42

Shade the graph to match the chart data above.

🍦 = 6

Blueberry Ice	🍦🍦🍦🍦🍦🍦
Mocha Cream	🍦🍦🍦🍦🍦🍦
Coconut Freeze	🍦🍦🍦🍦🍦🍦
Cherry Blizzard	🍦🍦🍦🍦🍦🍦

7

Apple School Supply		ABC School Supply	
10 pencils	$5.00	5 pencils	$2.00
notebook	$12.50	2 notebooks	$26.00
writing tablets	3 for $3.75	writing tablets	2 for $3.50

Raul needs to buy 1 pencil, 2 notebooks, and 5 writing tablets for school. Which store will save him the most money on these items? _____

8

The plastic lamp weighs about

_____

grams.

grams

9

○
○
○
○

10 Which number shows 9 hundred thousands, 25 ten thousands, and 7 tens?

1,150,070

900,250,070

9,257

925,070

Name

Day #1

Which number shows 2 million, 7 hundred thousands, 8 ten thousands, 4 tens, and 3 ones?

○ 3,780,043

○ 2,780,043

○ 3,878,403

○ 2,170,800,443

How many vertices are in the figures below?

_____

_____

Luigi sold a total of 1,321 raffle tickets in 3 weeks. He sold 467 tickets the first week and 299 tickets the second week. How many tickets did Luigi sell in the third week?

_____

```
  52
x 33
```

```
  28
x 56
```

Day #2

Write the fraction and the decimal shown by each model.

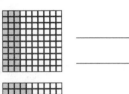

_____

_____

_____

Which number could be a remainder when dividing by 9?

○ 12

○ 7

○ 9

Which number could be a remainder when dividing by 3?

○ 10

○ 5

○ 1

Floyd and Kyle have 17 Super Pounce video games, 13 Blasto Control video games, and 20 Constellation video games. If they played each game for 30 minutes, could they play all the games in one day? _____

_____

○○✳✳✳✗✗
✭✓✭✓○○✳

Which series below would continue the pattern? _____

A. ✳✳✳✗✭✓

B. ✗✗✭✓✭✓

C. ✳✳✗✗✭✓

Day #3

Write the number that is 100 more than

234,967 _____

529,920 _____

862,425 _____

999,901 _____

---

1 cup = 8 ounces
1 pint = 2 cups
1 quart = 2 pints
1 gallon = 4 quarts

3 gallons = _____ quarts

5 pints = _____ cups

8 quarts = _____ pints

1 quart = _____ ounces

Write the number words.

2,450,137

_____

_____

_____

5,320,664

_____

_____

_____

$6\overline{)727}$

$4\overline{)838}$

Day #4

red = 36   green = 48
blue = 24   black = 12

To correctly color the pie graph so that it matches the above data, each section must stand for the same number. Determine that number, then color in the graph.

each part = _____

Mystery Numbers

A = 18 – (D x D)

B = C ÷ 4

C = D + A

D = the remainder of 47 ÷ 9

A = _____

B = _____

C = _____

D = _____

On Tuesday, Jet Air sold 45,951 airline tickets. Concourse Flights sold 31,764 tickets, and Miami Intrastate sold 18,752 tickets. What is the best estimate of the number of tickets sold by all 3 airlines?

○ 100,000 tickets

○ 125,000 tickets

○ 150,000 tickets

A [L L B B B]

B [L L L L B]

The chances of drawing an L are

○ equal between box A and B

○ less with box B

○ 2 times greater with box B

Assessment

1

$$\begin{array}{r} 98 \\ \times\ 52 \\ \hline \end{array} \qquad \begin{array}{r} 41 \\ \times\ 61 \\ \hline \end{array}$$

2

$9\overline{)748}$

3 CompuCom made 55,210 computer chips in March, 71,560 chips in April, and 66,102 chips in May. What is the best estimate of the number of computer chips made in all three months?

○ 250,000   ○ 150,000
○ 200,000   ○ 100,000

4 Megan's Girl Scout troop collected 1,072 pounds of aluminum cans last summer. In June, they collected 397 pounds and in July they collected 289 pounds. How many pounds of aluminum cans did they collect in August? _____

5 Which number could be a remainder when dividing by 4?

○ 7   ○ 2
○ 8   ○ 10

Which number could be a remainder when dividing by 8?

○ 7   ○ 16
○ 9   ○ 10

6 Write the number that is 100 less than

782,945 _____

541,099 _____

610,056 _____

7 Which number shows 6 millions, 29 hundred thousands, 6 thousands, 1 ten, and 5 ones?

○ 6,296,015

○ 8,960,015

○ 6,290,615

○ 82,900,105

8 How many vertices are in the figures below?

_____

_____

9 Elliot has a playoff game on Saturday at 4:00. This week, he has offered to do 3 chores for his grandmother, 5 chores for his mom, and 2 chores for his dad. Each chore takes about 30 minutes. Will he have time to do all the chores and still make it to the game on time if he gets up at 10:00? _____

10 Write the fraction and the decimal for each model.

_____

_____

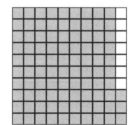

_____

_____

Day #1

Which number has a larger digit in the hundreds place than in the ten thousands place?

○ 3,928,743

○ 5,190,812

○ 6,278,421

○ 2,593,928

A square has 4 lines of symmetry.

How many lines of symmetry does a hexagon have? ___

Kalyn is baking 7 batches of cookies for the church social. Each batch uses the same amount of sugar. If she uses a total of 28 cups of sugar, which equation would tell the cups of sugar needed for each batch?

○ 7 x 28

○ 28 ÷ 7

○ 28 + 7

○ 28 – 7

```
  8,679
  4,527
+ 6,382
```

```
  622
x  52
```

Day #2

Write the decimal shown by each model.

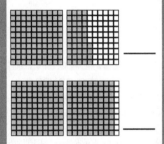

_____

_____

Which equation below best expresses the quotient for a number fact that equals 5?

○ 1 + 4 = 5

○ 25 – 20 = 5

○ 5 x 1 = 5

○ 25 ÷ 5 = 5

Mrs. Ganzer spends an hour doing laundry, 45 minutes vacuuming, a half-hour dusting, and 25 minutes mopping when she cleans house. How long does it take her to complete her housework? _____

Which series continues the pattern? _____

A. ✂✿✌

B. ★✌✂

C. ✂✿✿

Day #3

Continue counting. Write the next six numbers.

739,995
739,996
739,997
_____
_____
_____
_____
_____
_____

Find the volume for each solid figure below.

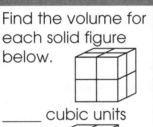

_____ cubic units

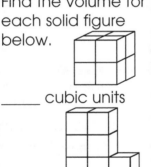

_____ cubic units

What number does the star best represent?

○ 12.5

○ 12.7

○ 13.5

○ 13.7

```
8)600
```

```
6)390
```

Day #4

orange = 40   green = 24
white = 16   purple = 48

To correctly color the pie graph so that it matches the above data, each section must stand for the same number. Determine that number, then color the graph.
each part
= _____

Tam's age is an even number less than 14. He is one-half his sister's age. His sister's age is a number between 16 and 24.

How old is Tam?_____

How old is his sister? _____

Casey's bead art set has 372 beads for each of 12 colors. She saw 23 more sets like hers in the craft store. Which is the best estimate for the number of beads in all the sets?

○ 80,000

○ 70,000

○ 60,000

○ 100,000

| 1 | 5 | 9 | 1 | 5 |

If these cards are shuffled and placed facedown, the chances of drawing a 1 are _____ to the chances of drawing a 5, and _____ times greater than the chances of drawing a 9.

Assessment

1

$$\begin{array}{r} 345 \\ \times\ 47 \end{array}$$

$$\begin{array}{r} 4,254 \\ 9,897 \\ +\ 6,579 \end{array}$$

2

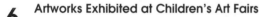

$$4\overline{)300}$$

3

✓ ✗ ✗ ✗ ▲
▲ ▲ ○

If these cards are shuffled and placed facedown, the chances of drawing an ✗ are _____ to the chances of drawing a ▲ and _____ times greater than drawing a ✓.

4

The letter A best represents what number?

○ 11.9   ○ 10.5

○ 11.5   ○ 10.7

5 Wayne is boxing fireworks for sale at his uncle's stand. Each box contains the same number. So far he has 210 fireworks in 7 boxes. Which equation would tell how many fireworks are in each box?

○ 210 + 7
○ 210 x 7
○ 210 − 7
○ 210 ÷ 7

6 **Artworks Exhibited at Children's Art Fairs**

1995 = 25   color white
1996 = 20   color green
1997 = 40   color blue
1998 = 35   color red

Color the pie graph to match the above data by determining the value of each section.   each part = _____

7 Mindy and her friends went to the county fair. They spent 1 hour and 20 minutes riding the rides. They played games at the booths for 45 minutes, visited the exhibits for a half-hour, then went into the fun house for 15 minutes before going home. How long did Mindy and her friends stay at the fair?

_____

8 Find the volume for the solid figures below.

_____ cubic units   _____ cubic units

9 Which numeral has a lesser digit in the hundred thousands place than in the tens place?

○ 5,836,170

○ 8,208,957

○ 6,530,659

○ 2,970,885

10 At the candy factory, the workers pack 47 chocolate delights in each box. They can pack about 53 boxes each hour. What is the best estimate of the number of chocolate delights packed in 8 hours?

○ 20,000

○ 21,000

○ 22,000

○ 23,000

Day #1

Which number has a lesser digit in the thousands place than in the ten millions place?

○ 347,928,743

○ 562,147,812

○ 620,213,401

○ 754,563,928

A square has 4 lines of symmetry

How many lines of symmetry does a pentagon have?

_____

What is the difference in length between a hiking trail 20,402 meters long and a trail 13,857 meters long? _____

321
x 52

$12\frac{15}{30}$

$6\frac{25}{30}$

+

Day #2

Add the decimals shown by each model.

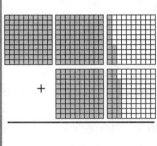

+

= _____

Tony's math grades are 85, 92, 95, 81, and 92.

What is his average grade in math?

_____

How can you make $1.27 using a minimal collection of these coins?

_____ nickels
_____ dimes
_____ pennies

How can you make $1.27 using a minimal collection of these coins?

_____ quarters
_____ pennies

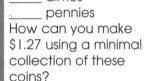

Shade in the next two squares to continue the pattern.

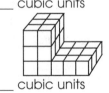

Day #3

Continue counting. Write the next six numbers.

995,985
995,990
995,995

_____
_____
_____
_____
_____
_____

Find the volume for each solid figure below.

_____ cubic units

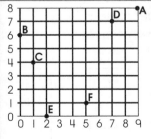

_____ cubic units

What number does the star best represent?

○ 13.25

○ 13.50

○ 13.75

○ 14.10

50)4,500

$25\frac{2}{12}$

$14\frac{10}{12}$
-

Day #4

Name the ordered pairs.

A _____   B _____
C _____   D _____
E _____   F _____

The area of the dining table is an even number. The desk is a square. The coffee table's length is three times its width. The end table's area is one-half of one of the other tables. Match the area to each table.

6 sq. ft. _____
20 sq. ft. _____
12 sq. ft. _____
16 sq. ft. _____

33,452,835 rounded to the nearest

10 = _____
1,000 = _____
100,000 = _____
1,000,000 =

_____

Subtract. Simplify the answer.

$11\frac{3}{9} - \frac{4}{9} =$ ____

$\frac{21}{5} - \frac{6}{5} =$ ____

$17\frac{3}{24} - 8 =$ ____

Assessment

1

$$345 \times 32$$ $$40\overline{)2,800}$$

2 Subtract and simplify the answer.

$$12\frac{3}{14} - 7\frac{10}{14} = \underline{\hspace{1cm}}$$

$$\frac{24}{8} - \frac{20}{8} = \underline{\hspace{1cm}}$$

3 6,251,481 rounded to the nearest

100 = _____

10,000 = _____

100,000 = _____

4 What is the difference in length between a highway 147,895 meters long and a highway 601,234 meters long? _____

5 What is Ray's average score in bowling? _____

Ray's Bowling Scores	
Game	Points per Game
1	102
2	98
3	129
4	201
5	80

6 Continue counting. Write the next six numbers.

895,680   _____

895,780   _____

895,880   _____

895,980   _____

_____

7 Which number has a digit of greater value in the hundred thousands place than in the ten millions place?

○ 875,836,170

○ 861,508,957

○ 651,530,659

○ 280,190,885

8 How many lines of symmetry are there for each figure?

Draw in the lines of symmetry.

____   ____   ____

9 How can you make $2.38 using a minimal collection of these coins? Write the amount for each coin.

quarters _____   nickels _____   pennies _____

How can you make $2.38 using a minimal collection of these coins? Write the amount for each coin.

half-dollars _____   quarters _____

dimes _____   pennies _____

10 Name the ordered pairs.

A _____

B _____

C _____

D _____

E _____

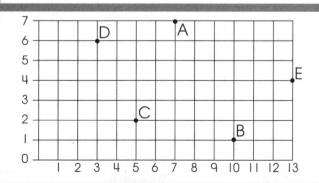

Name **Week # 24**

Day #1

In 1978, the most expensive coin was a $20.00 gold piece. Hal read that the gold piece sold for an approximate dollar amount that had an 8 in the tens place, a 4 in the thousands place, a 5 in the ones place, and a 3 in the hundred thousands place. What was the price of the coin?

______

Label the lines I for intersecting, PA for parallel, and P for perpendicular.

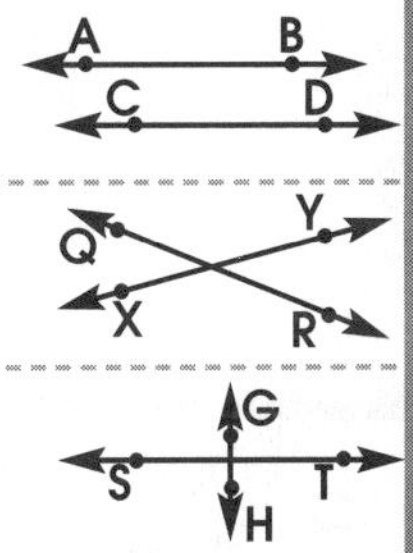

______

______

______

The greatest oil gusher was at Spindletop, Texas in 1901. It yielded about 810,459 barrels of oil in 9 days. About how many barrels of oil did this oil gusher produce each day?

______

$$\begin{array}{r} 605 \\ \times\ 85 \\ \hline \end{array}$$

$$20\overline{)453}$$

Day #2

Subtract the decimals shown by each model.

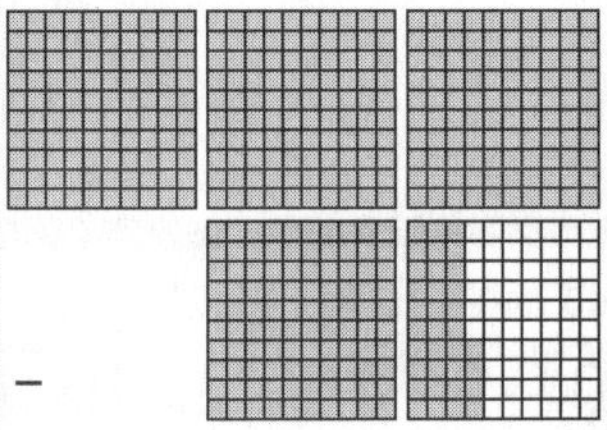

–

=

______

Circle common factors for each number pair.

4, 16

2 4 8 10 16 20

10, 20

2 3 4 5 10 20

18, 36

2 3 4 6 9 12 18

Oscar earns $5.25 per hour working part time at the grocery store. Last week he worked 4 hours a day for 6 days. How much did Oscar earn last week?

______

9, 11, 15, 23, 39, 7

What is the rule for the pattern above? (Hint: use two operations.)

______

______

Day #3

Japanese Cities Populations 1977	
Tokyo	8,112,000
Osaka	3,276,000
Yokohama	2,601,000
Sapporo	2,162,000
Nagoya	1,719,000

List the cities in order from least to greatest population. ______

______

______

Using the lines of symmetry, find the perimeter of this hexagon.

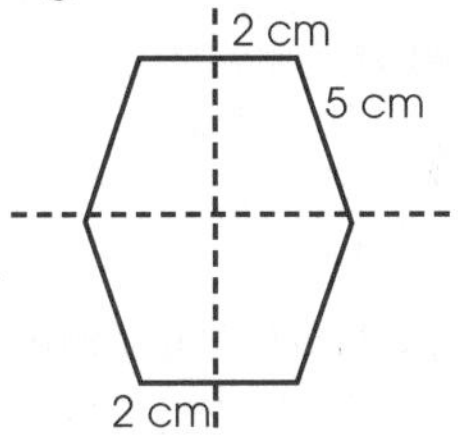

perimeter = ______ cm

The continent of Asia has a land mass of forty-three million, nine hundred seventy-five thousand square kilometers. This number is written in numerals as

- ◯ 43,975,000
- ◯ 430,975
- ◯ 439,750,000
- ◯ 43,975

$$\begin{array}{r} 4.37 \\ 6.22 \\ +\ 4.50 \\ \hline \end{array} \qquad \begin{array}{r} 9.82 \\ 3.41 \\ +\ 7.25 \\ \hline \end{array}$$

$$\begin{array}{r} 9.82 \\ -\ 3.25 \\ \hline \end{array} \qquad \begin{array}{r} 8.12 \\ -\ 6.78 \\ \hline \end{array}$$

Day #4

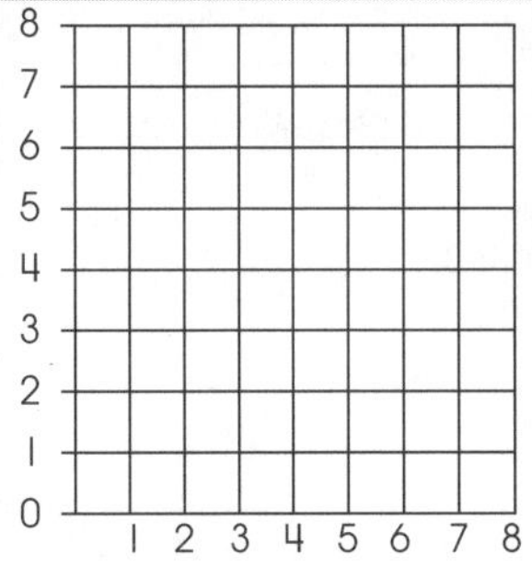

Plot these symbols.

✖ = (8, 7) ◆ = (0, 2)

▲ = (4, 6) ■ = (5, 1)

Popeye Pig ate over 100 peanuts, which was twice as many peanuts as Pinky Pig ate. Pinky ate a number of peanuts that is divisible by 7. Petunia Pig ate 11 more peanuts than Pinky. The number she ate is an odd number between 60 and 70. How many peanuts did each pig eat?

Popeye ______ Pinky ______

Petunia ______

The world's largest park is the Wood Buffalo Park in Canada. It is 19,362 times larger than the world's oldest park in London which covers 577 acres. Which equation best estimates the size of the Canadian park?

- ◯ 21,400 x 700
- ◯ 20,000 x 600
- ◯ 19,000 x 600
- ◯ 20,000 x 400

$9\frac{19}{42} + 17\frac{25}{42} =$ ______

$52\frac{12}{30} - 25\frac{22}{30} =$ ______

$31\frac{1}{15} - 18\frac{9}{15} =$ ______

Assessment

1

403
x 75

60⟌385

2

3.05
2.61
+ 9.85

12.21
- 9.85

3   4, 17, 56, 173, 524

What is the rule for the pattern?

(Hint: use two operations.)

_____

4 In square miles, the country of India has an area of one million, two hundred twenty-nine thousand, seven hundred thirty-seven. This number is written
- ○ 12,297,037
- ○ 1,229,737
- ○ 122,973,007

5 During one week in August, the Icy Freeze Shop used 140,210 ice cubes to make snow cones. If the Icy Freeze Shop used the same number of ice cubes each day, how many ice cubes were used daily?

_____

6 Plot the symbols.

✔ = (10, 7)

✚ = (1, 8)

■ = (0, 3)

○ = (5, 5)

7 Evan spent $9.48 a week to rent videos. How much did he spend in 8 weeks? _____

8 Using the lines of symmetry, find the perimeter of this figure.

perimeter = _____ mm

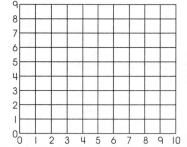

5 mm
←10 mm
↓20 mm
5 mm

9 Scott was looking at a warehouse catalog for ordering music cassette tapes, compact disks, and albums. The number of items available through the catalog had a 7 in the ten thousands place, a 5 in the hundreds place, a 9 in the hundred thousands place, and a 6 in the ones place. How many items were in the catalog? _____

10 In the 1890s, railroad passenger travel was estimated to be about 11,848,000 passenger miles. In 1974, the number of passenger miles was 67 times that amount. Which equation best estimates the number of passenger miles traveled in 1974?

- ○ 1,890 x 11,000 million
- ○ 60 x 11 million
- ○ 70 x 12 million
- ○ 60 x 10 million

Name

Day #1

Susan read that one of the longest toy balloon flights achieved a record length in miles. The balloon traveled an approximate distance that had a 1 in the hundreds place, a 5 in the tens place, a 9 in the thousands place, a 7 in the hundredths place, and a 5 in the tenths place. How far did the balloon travel?

_____ miles

Label each figure by writing the letter inside the figure.
A. a pentagon with 2 right angles
B. a quadrilateral with 1 right angle
C. an equilateral triangle
D. a right triangle

One of the largest living trees, the General Sherman tree, is a Sequoia in California. It is about 272.3 feet tall. The tallest redwood tree is about 367.8 feet tall. What is the difference in height between the two trees? _____

923
x 381

50⟌1,532

Day #2

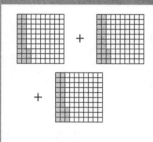

= 3 x 0.23 = _____

What is the greatest common factor for

12 and 16 _____

20 and 30 _____

36 and 35 _____

How many?

8 hours = _____ minutes

3 days = _____ hours

1 hour = _____ seconds

one-quarter hour = _____ minutes

1 year = _____ hours

Create your own pattern.

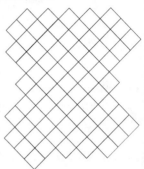

Day #3

Write the decimals in order from least to greatest.

3.45 3.5 3.82
3.02 3.1 3.67

_____ _____

_____ _____

_____ _____

Use the grid to enlarge the top figure to two times its size.

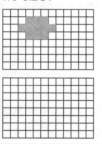

In 1970, a car, "The Blue Flame," achieved an average speed of six hundred twenty-seven and twenty-nine hundredths miles per hour. This number is written

○ 62,729.0029

○ 627.29

○ 627.029

34.97
16.20
+ 54.03

30.02
− 16.18

42.12
− 29.90

19.02
73.69
+ 13.50

Day #4

Number of Girls & Boys Enrolled at School

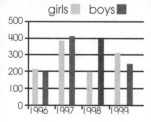

1. During which year was the enrollment for girls and boys about the same? _____

Use the graph at the left.

2. In which years was the enrollment less for girls than boys? _____

3. In which year was the enrollment for girls about 390? _____

4. In which years was the enrollment for girls about 200?

_____ _____

Aidan has 4 collections: rocks, shells, stamps, and marbles. Each collection has between 20 and 50 items. What is a reasonable total for all the items in his collection?

○ 75

○ 520

○ 150

In a meter race, Alan ran 3 times as far as Cathy. Cathy ran one-half as far as David. David's total meters run was a multiple of 7 less than 50. Becky ran 21 times less than the number of meters run by Alan. How many meters did each student run?

Alan _____
Becky _____
Cathy _____
David _____

Assessment

1

726
× 438

80)5,625

2

71.90
36.70
+ 19.09

31.04
– 17.18

3 Emil played hoops 5 times. Each time he made between 10 and 40 baskets. What is a reasonable total for the baskets made by Emil?

○ 205   ○ 185

○ 50   ○ 20

4 In 1965, an American aviator flew his plane at speeds of about 3,331.5 kilometers per hour. In 1962, a Russian aviator flew his plane at about 2,680.00 kilometers per hour. What is the difference in speed between the two flights?

_____ kph

5 Circle the common factors for the pairs of numbers.

10, 15

2   3   5

24, 40

2   3   5   6   8   10

6 Write the decimals in order from greatest to least.

7.28   7.02   7.82   7.08   7.8   8.1

_____, _____, _____,

_____, _____, _____

7 Manuel was reading that one of the tallest structures in the world is a radio tower in Poland. The tower's height in feet has a 1 in the hundreds place, a 2 in the tens place, a 2 in the thousands place, and an 8 in the tenths place. Write the height of the building. _____

8 Label each figure. Write the label inside each figure.
  A. pentagon with 2 right angles
  B. quadrilateral with 2 right angles
  C. right triangle

____   ____   ____

9 How many?

6 hours = _____ minutes

5 days = _____ hours

one-quarter hour = _____ minutes

1 hour = _____ seconds

10 Use the models to multiply the decimals.

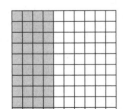

× 2 = _____

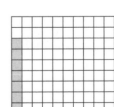

× 5 = _____

Which number has a 5 in the ten thousands place, a 3 in the hundreds place, an 8 in the millions place, and a 6 in the hundredths place?

○ 850,308.60

○ 8,005,308.30

○ 8,057,308.06

○ 85,360,016.6

Label each triangle.

A. right triangle

B. scalene triangle

C. acute triangle

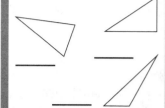

_____   _____

_____

_____

Each student in Mr. Hernandez's class brought $3.25 for the end of the year pizza party. The party cost $78.00. What information is needed to determine whether there will be enough money? _____

_____

145
x □
2900

51
□)2,550

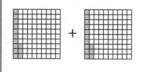

+

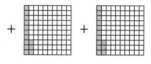

+   +

_____ x 4 = _____

If 30 is 4 times less than a number, which equation could be used to find the number?

○ 30 x 4 = n

○ 30 ÷ 4 = n

○ 30 + 4 = n

○ 30 − 4 = n

Ikito spends $4\frac{1}{2}$ hours practicing his violin each week. He has practiced for $1\frac{3}{4}$ hours this week. How many more minutes does he need to practice? _____

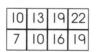

| 10 | 13 | 19 | 22 |
| 7 | 10 | 16 | 19 |

What two numbers come next in this pattern?

Write the decimals in order from greatest to least.

12.85   13.2   12.08
13.02   13.50   12.6

_____ , _____ ,

_____ , _____ ,

_____ , _____

Use the grid to enlarge the top figure three times its size.

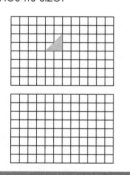

A   B C   D
35   36   37   38

Match using the number line.

_____ 37.21

_____ 35.4

_____ 37.89

_____ 36.5

5,340
− □
3,702

9,846
+ □
14,772

Average Minutes to Complete 1K Race

Jim ▪ Ted □

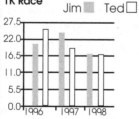

27.5
22.0
16.5
11.0
5.5
0.0
   1996   1997   1998

Which chart to the right best matches the data on the above graph? _____

		Jim	Ted
A	1996	20.2	25.5
	1997	24.7	20.5
	1998	19.21	18.85
B	1996	16.5	27.5
	1997	20.7	20.5
	1998	11.21	12.85
C	1996	22.0	25.5
	1997	28.7	20.5
	1998	19.21	5.85

Each year Rita has between 21 and 45 classmates. What is a reasonable total for the number of classmates she had in grades one through six?

○ 150

○ 250

○ 350

For a community food drive, Mrs. Witt needed to pack 438 cans of vegetables. She can pack 40 cans in each box. What is the least number of boxes she can use to pack all the cans? _____

Assessment

1

$$\begin{array}{r} 225 \\ \times\ \boxed{} \\ \hline 11{,}250 \end{array}$$

$$\boxed{}\,\overline{)\,2{,}100\,}^{\,30}$$

2

$$\begin{array}{r} 7{,}109 \\ -\ \boxed{} \\ \hline 4{,}387 \end{array}$$

$$\begin{array}{r} 8{,}298 \\ +\ \boxed{} \\ \hline 13{,}105 \end{array}$$

3

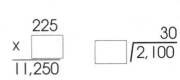

11	18	25	39
2	9	14	30

Which two numbers are missing from this pattern? ⬚

4

Match using the number line.

_____ 44.10   _____ 42.92

_____ 44.5   _____ 43.75

_____ 42.25

5 Several friends went to Six Flags Amusement Park. Their total entrance fee was $264.00. What information do you need to find out the entrance fee for each person?

_____

6

Average Miles on Road Race Video Game

☐ Sam   ▨ Joe

Circle the chart that best matches the graph.

Game	1	2	3
Sam	53.5	22.1	8.79
Joe	12.3	38.2	17.5

Game	1	2	3
Sam	52.2	27.9	8.79
Joe	19.3	45.2	22.3

7 Paula's goal is to jog for 2 hours and 45 minutes a week. So far this week, she has jogged for $\frac{3}{4}$ of an hour. How many more minutes does she need to jog to meet her weekly goal? _____

8 Use the empty grid to enlarge this shape two times.

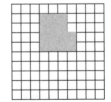

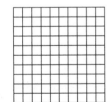

9 Which number has a 5 in the tens place, a 7 in the ten thousands place, a 6 in the millions place, and a 4 in the hundredths place?

○ 5,760,401

○ 6,270,052.04

○ 5,670,219.4

○ 6,870,059.40

10 Erin goes swimming between 52 and 105 times each summer. What would be a reasonable total of the times she has gone swimming over the last 6 years?

○ 525

○ 725

○ 825

○ 225

Day #1

Name the place and the value of the 4 in each number.

34,127 _____

_____

41,980 _____

_____

Iso means bend. *Equi* means same. *Ska* means uneven. Use the clues to number each triangle.

A. isosceles

B. equilateral _____

C. scalene

_____   _____

Soccer camp costs $125.00 per team. The team washed 50 cars to earn money for camp. What information is needed to determine whether they earned enough money? _____

_____

$86\frac{25}{27}$

$+ \ 48\frac{11}{27}$

$73\frac{7}{49}$

$- \ 29\frac{14}{49}$

Day #2

Write the decimal for each model.

_____   _____

If 120 is 3 times more than a number, which equation could be used to find the number?

○ 120 × 3 = n

○ 120 ÷ 3 = n

○ 120 + 3 = n

○ 120 − 3 = n

Fernando worked after school to save money for a video game that cost $63.00. At the end of 3 months, he had enough to buy the game. How much money did he save each month? _____

_____

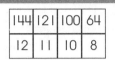

144	121	100	64
12	11	10	8

What two numbers are missing in this pattern?

Day #3

List the students in order from highest to lowest math average.

Math Average	
Cathy	81.55
Paul	97.2
Roberto	88.25
Hakeem	96.7
Leslie	92.5

_____

_____

_____

_____

Enlarge the top figure two times.

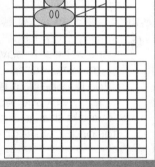

```
   A  B  C     D
←──●──●──●─────●──→
  73  74  75  76
```

Match using the number line.

_____ 73.92

_____ 75.75

_____ 73.08

_____ 74.42

$4,681$

$- \ \boxed{}$

$1,443$

876

$+ \ \boxed{}$

$1,862$

Day #4

Value of Mineral Produced Billions (in dollars)

■ U.S.A.
▨ China
□ S. Africa
▤ Saudi Arabia

Which chart to the right best matches the data on the graph above? _____

A	U.S.A.	62.27
	China	16.7
	S. Africa	8.51
	Saudi Arabia	19.42
B	U.S.A.	8.51
	China	16.7
	S. Africa	62.27
	Saudi Arabia	19.42
C	U.S.A.	19.42
	China	8.51
	S. Africa	16.7
	Saudi Arabia	62.27

Movie Opening	$ Gross
Dino Island	$37,539
Tidal Terror	$9,210
Star Invasion	$69,510

What is the best estimate of the money grossed by all three movies?

○ $120,000

○ $155,000

○ $250,000

The cooks at the Grand Hotel are preparing a special shrimp dish for their menu. They will need 729 shrimp. The shrimp comes in bulk packages of 80. What is the least number of packages the cooks can buy? _____

Assessment

1

$$62\frac{31}{60}$$
$$+ 38\frac{29}{60}$$

$$73\frac{3}{64}$$
$$- 28\frac{35}{64}$$

2

$$5,802$$
$$- \boxed{}$$
$$\overline{1,349}$$

$$4,307$$
$$+ \boxed{}$$
$$\overline{11,464}$$

3 What is the best estimate of the money grossed in ticket sales for all three concerts?

Ponytails Concert	$ Gross Ticket Sales
Houston	$21,135
Chicago	$59,421
Seattle	$77,982

○ $160,000
○ $140,000
○ $150,000
○ $130,000

4 Ms. Alipour needed $236.00 to buy an air conditioner for the kennels at her pet grooming shop. She groomed 12 dogs. What information is needed to find out if this would be enough money to buy the air conditioner? _____

5 If 450 is 3 times more than a number, which equation could be used to find the number?

○ 450 x 3 = n
○ 450 + 3 = n
○ 450 ÷ 3 = n
○ 450 – 3 = n

6 List the competitors' names in order from the highest to the lowest average score.

Average Scores on Diving Competition	
Rudi	72.3
Brook	88.21
Lindsay	88.57
Milly	71.9
Cecily	72.71

_____
_____
_____
_____
_____

7 Name the place and the value for the 7 in each number below.

72,509 _____

_____

29,709 _____

_____

8 Match.

A. equilateral   B. isosceles   C. scalene

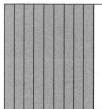

_____   _____   _____

9 Tiffany worked at her father's florist shop after school to save money for a summer gymnastic camp. Tuition for the camp was $108.00. She was paid the same amount for each week she worked and at the end of 9 weeks she had enough money to pay the tuition. How much did she earn each week?

_____

10 Write the decimal for each model.

_____   _____   _____   _____

Name the place and the value of the 5 in each number.

520,347 _____

_____

_____

5,201,968 _____

_____

_____

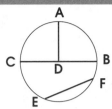

Name each line segment.

radius _____

chord _____

diameter _____

Alleha weighs 89 pounds. To find the weight of her baby brother, she held him as she weighed herself again. This time the scale showed 102 pounds. How much does Alleha's baby brother weigh?

_____

31,094
− 867

20,532
− 785

Day #1

Shade in and write an equivalent decimal for each model.

0.7 = _____

0.3 = _____

Two hundred forty drivers competed in the 8-day road rally. On average, how many drivers raced each day?

_____

The spirit club sold banners to earn money for a party. They sold 108 banners at $3.00 each. How much money did the spirit club earn?

_____

Tim and his friends designed paper airplanes. Their best model could fly 103 inches. The next day, they improved the model so it could fly 112 inches. If the improvement continues in this pattern, how far will the plane fly on the fifth day? _____ inches

Day #2

Write >, <, or = to compare.

52.13 ☐ 52.3

10.10 ☐ 10.1

75.42 ☐ 75.49

23.08 ☐ 23.8

Each ☐ = 3 feet
What is the perimeter of the shape? _____ ft.
What is the area? _____ sq. ft.

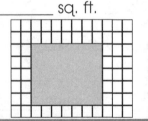

Match.
A. 74.2   B. 72.04
C. 72.4   D. 70.42

_____ seventy-two and four-hundredths

_____ seventy and forty-two-hundredths

_____ seventy-four and two-tenths

_____ seventy-two and four-tenths

215,743
315,094
+ 867,255

8,200,999
+ 12,836,487

Day #3

Reforestation Project

Park	Number of New Trees
King	
Ford	
Taft	
Bush	

each = 25 trees

The forestry service wishes to plant 850 new trees in these 4 parks. Shade the graph to show how many more trees are needed in Bush Park to meet this goal.

wrapping papers

ribbons

Kalyn is wrapping gifts. Using the above ribbons and paper, how many different combinations can she make? _____

Round each number to the nearest tenth.

36.42 _____

92.19 _____

77.87 _____

14.64 _____

❀ ❁ ❀ ❀ ❋ ❋

In the above group of flowers, the odds of picking a ❀ over a ❁ are 3 to 1. What are the odds of picking a ❀ over a ❋?

_____ to _____

Day #4

Assessment

1

47,084
– 31,267

2

831,457
217,886
+ 504,108

3 Round each number to the nearest tenth.

84.12 _____

15.58 _____

27.07 _____

4 Match.
A. 94.4   B. 94.7   C. 94.07   D. 94.47

_____ ninety-four and seven-hundredths

_____ ninety-four and seven-tenths

_____ ninety-four and forty-seven-hundredths

_____ ninety-four and four-tenths

5 Andy wanted to find the weight of a pumpkin he bought. When he got on the scale alone, he weighed 92 pounds. When he weighed again, holding the pumpkin, the scale read 100 pounds. How much did his pumpkin weigh? _____

6

Park	Number of Bears Collared
Yellowstone	
Yosemite	
Smokey Mt.	
Glacier	

each ▨ = 20

To study the habitats of bears, the park service plans to radio collar 620 bears in these 4 parks. Shade the graph to show how many more bears need to be collared in Yosemite to meet the total.

7 Papers Designs

Pavet was designing covers for his journals. Using the above papers and designs, how many different combinations of covers can he make? _____

8 What is the perimeter of the shape? _____ ft.
What is the area? _____ sq. ft.

each ☐ = 4 feet

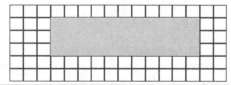

9 Name the place and the value for the 2 in each numeral below.

2,631,980 _____

_____

8,219,443 _____

_____

10 ☆☆☆☆○○○   ▲▲▲▲▲▲☐☐

The odds of drawing a ☆ over a ○ are 4 to 3 with the above group of shapes.

With the above group of shapes, the odds of drawing a ▲ over a ☐ are _____ to _____.

Complete the place value chart.

A		C	D	E	F		

millions   tens ones

A = _____
place

C = _____
place

E = _____ place

Match.

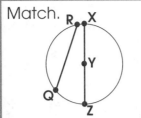

$\overline{XY}$ _____   A. diameter

$\overline{QR}$ _____   B. radius

$\overline{XZ}$ _____   C. chord

Each of the 26 students in art class has a set of 18 watercolor pens. How many watercolor pens do they have altogether? _____

$$211,005 - 24,146$$

$$98,778 + 76,845$$

Write an equivalent fraction.

1.9 = _____

0.20 = _____

9.45 = _____

4.07 = _____

Complete the chart to find some multiples for each numeral.

x	4	6	8
2			
3			
4			
5			
6			
7			
8			
9			

Circle the common multiples.

Although this clock is missing the minute hand, what is the best estimate of the time it shows?

○ 4:30

○ 3:02

○ 3:45

Ada was collecting plant specimens for a botany class. On the first day she collected 23 specimens. The next day, she collected 3 more specimens than the first day. If she continues the same pattern, how many plant specimens total will she have on the fifth day? _____

Write >, <, or = to compare.

71.93 [ ] 71.930

18.2 [ ] 18.035

98.52 [ ] 98.541

43.17 [ ] 43.189

Each ☐ = 4 square feet

What is the area of the shape? _____ sq. ft.

What is the approximate perimeter? _____ ft.

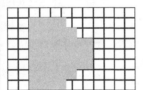

Write the number word for each.

35.607 _____

_____

29.35 _____

_____

$$5,421 \times 33$$

$$7{\overline{)21,426}}$$

Number of 100% Homework Papers

Abe	22
Kate	20
Jen	32
Todd	30

Complete the bar graph for the chart data.

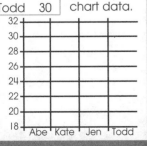

Using the colors red, pink, purple, and white only one time in each row, how many different colored rows of hearts can you make? _____

Round each number to the nearest whole number.

21.032 _____

87.67 _____

45.02 _____

99.506 _____

7	7	7	7	7

3	3	3	3	

If the above group of cards is shuffled and placed facedown, what are the odds of picking a 7 over a 3? _____ to _____.

1

212,003
− 87,136

2

7,214
x   25

3 Round each number to the nearest whole number.

98.345 _____

27.702 _____

82.027 _____

4 Each of the 34 children in the City Celebration Parade carried 9 flag-shaped balloons. How many balloons were carried by all the children in the parade? _____

5 Complete the chart. Circle the common multiples of 3, 6, and 9.

x	2	3	4	5	6	7	8	9	10
3									
6									
9									

6 Write >, <, or = to compare.

39.43 ☐ 39.048

47.098 ☐ 47.98

81.3 ☐ 81.300

7 Complete the place value chart.

A	B	millions	D	E	F	G	tens	ones

A = _____ place

D = _____ place

F = _____ place

G = _____ place

8 Match.

A. diameter
B. radius
C. chord

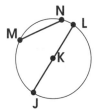

MN _____

KL _____

JL _____

9 Although the minute hand is missing, what is the best estimate of the time shown on this clock?

○ 11:15

○ 6:00

○ 12:45

○ 11:58

10 Complete the bar graph for the chart data.

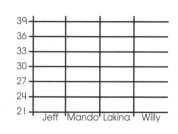

Super Citizen Stars Earned

Jeff	36	★
Mando	30	★
Lakina	33	★
Willy	24	★

Day #1

If a 3 is followed by 8 zeros, the 3 is in the _____ place.

If a 7 is followed by 6 zeros, the 7 is in the _____ place.

If polygons are congruent, the corresponding or matching angles are also congruent. For example:

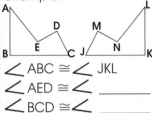

∠ ABC ≅ ∠ JKL

∠ AED ≅ ∠ _____

∠ BCD ≅ ∠ _____

Kevin's remote control bi-plane can fly 3.42 meters high. Danny's plane can fly 4.021 meters high. How much higher can Danny's plane fly?

_____

345.043
− 127.127

358.79
+ 668.402

Day #2

A pizza has 12 slices. Julio ate 8 slices. Which fraction describes the portion Julio ate.

○ $\frac{1}{2}$　○ $\frac{3}{4}$　○ $\frac{2}{3}$

Which fraction describes the portion of pizza that was left?

○ $\frac{1}{2}$　○ $\frac{1}{3}$　○ $\frac{1}{12}$

(6 x 2) x 5 is equivalent to

○ (6 x 2) + 5

○ (6 ÷ 2) x 5

○ 6 x (2 x 5)

(9 + 4) + 8 is equivalent to

○ (9 x 4) + 8

○ 9 + (4 + 8)

○ 9 x (8 x 4)

Although this clock is missing the minute hand, what is the best estimate of the time it shows?

○ 8:20

○ 8:59

○ 9:15

Kalui caught 27 fish. On the first day, he sold 7 of them at the market. If each day after, he sells 1 less fish than on the day before, on what day will he have no fish left to sell?

_____

Day #3

Number of Drinks Sold

List the drinks sold from least to greatest.

1. _____　2. _____
3. _____　4. _____
5. _____　6. _____

Which is a way to find the area of this shape?

○ (5 + 4) + (4 − 1)

○ (5 x 1) + (5 x 2)

○ (4 x 3) + (1 x 1)

○ (5 + 3) + (4 + 3)

Write the number word for each number.

71.032 _____

_____

_____

12.05 _____

_____

_____

9,876
x　 63

9⟌45,452

Day #4

Weekly Temperatures

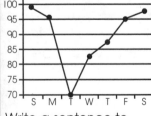

Write a sentence to summarize the graph data. _____

_____

_____

If 2n = 54 ÷ 9

n = ☐

If 5n = 26 + 4

n = ☐

If 3n = 30 − 3

n = ☐

Jiffy's Pizza is running a special of 2 pizzas for $15.00. Which would be a reasonable cost of 7 pizzas?

○ $30.00

○ $40.00

○ $50.00

○ $60.00

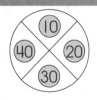

If all the colored circles on the dart board are the same size, the probability of hitting a 20 (expressed as a fraction) is _____

Assessment

1
$$582.74$$
$$+ 217.806$$

2
$$3\overline{)27,182}$$

3 Skinny the clown had 20 balloons to pass out at the circus. He gave the first child entering the big top 6 balloons. If he gives each of the next children 1 less than the child before, with which child will Skinny be out of balloons? _____

4 Write the number word for each number.

24.017 _____

_____

10.51 _____

_____

30.6 _____

_____

5 Miss Tamira was measuring walls in the museum for a new tapestry exhibit. The west wall was 7.13 meters wide and the north wall was 9.06 meters wide. How much wider was the north wall? _____

6 Write a sentence to summarize the graph data.

_____
_____
_____
_____
_____

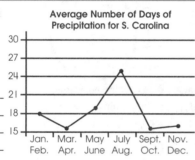

Average Number of Days of Precipitation for S. Carolina

30
27
24
21
18
15

Jan. Mar. May July Sept. Nov.
Feb. Apr. June Aug. Oct. Dec.

7
If $7n = 84 \div 12$; $n = \boxed{}$

If $5n = 100 - 25$; $n = \boxed{}$

If $9n = 27 + 18$; $n = \boxed{}$

8 Which shows a way to find the area of this shape?

○ $(8 \times 2) + (8 \times 2)$

○ (8×6)

○ $(8 \times 4) - (8 \times 2)$

○ $(8 \times 6) - (4 \times 2)$

9 If a 7 is followed by 4 zeros, the 7 is in the _____ place.

If a 2 is followed by 9 zeros, the 2 is in the _____ place.

10 Easy Feet Shoe Store is having a sale: 5 pairs of shoes for $40.00. Mrs. Sans, Mrs. King, and Mrs. Boyd bought 12 pairs of shoes for their families. What would be a reasonable cost of the 12 pairs of shoes the women bought?

○ $50.00   ○ $100.00

○ $150.00   ○ $200.00

Day #1

Which number has a 4 in the ten billions place?

- ○ 45,0872,501
- ○ 421,704,623
- ○ 475,189,080,225
- ○ 248,095,667,120

Which are corresponding angles?

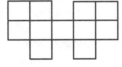

∠____ ≅ ∠____

Marquis had 50 jawbreaker candies. He wanted to keep 2 for his little brother and share the rest equally with 8 of his friends. How many jawbreakers will each of his friends receive? _____

$$121,092 \\ - \ \ 95,095$$

$$622,173 \\ 415,669 \\ + \ 323,355$$

Day #2

Mr. Prine bought a book of 36 stamps. He used 9 to mail some letters. Which fraction describes the portion of stamps he used?

○ $\frac{1}{2}$ ○ $\frac{3}{4}$ ○ $\frac{1}{4}$

What fraction of stamps was left?

○ $\frac{1}{2}$ ○ $\frac{3}{4}$ ○ $\frac{1}{36}$

(9 x 3) + (9 x 5)
is equivalent to

- ○ 9 x (3 x 5)
- ○ (9 x 9) + (3 x 5)
- ○ 9 x (3 + 5)

(9 ÷ 3) + (15 ÷ 3)
is equivalent to

- ○ (9 x 3) ÷ 5
- ○ (9 + 15) ÷ 3
- ○ (9 x 5) ÷ 6

Andrea bought 3 sets of fingernail tattoos for $3.25 a set, including tax. She gave the clerk a $20 bill. How much change did Andrea receive?

_____

Tyler went hiking in the forest. He carried a pack with 124 small pebbles. To help him find his way back, he dropped pebbles every 5 meters. At the first 5 meters, he dropped 4 pebbles. At 10 meters, he dropped 8 pebbles. If he continues dropping twice the number of pebbles, how far can he hike into the forest until he runs out of pebbles? _____

Day #3

Average Daily Temperature °F

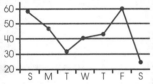

List the days in order from the highest to lowest temperature.

1. _____ 2. _____
3. _____ 4. _____
5. _____ 6. _____
7. _____

Which is a way to find the area of this shape?

- ○ 2 x (2 x 2) + 3 x (1 x 1)
- ○ (2 + 2) + (2 + 2) + 12
- ○ (5 x 2) + (5 x 2)
- ○ (4 + 4) − 3

Which number does point S best represent?

- ○ 65.2
- ○ 64.2
- ○ 64.6
- ○ 64.9
- ○ none of the above

$$315 \\ \times \ 214$$

$$22 \overline{)675}$$

Day #4

Pat's Keyboarding Scores

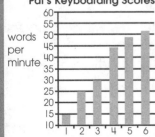

Write a sentence to summarize the graph data. _____
_____

If $n + 5 = 6 \times 6$

$n =$ ☐

If $n - 4 = 30 + 4$

$n =$ ☐

If $n \div 2 = 12 \div 6$

$n =$ ☐

Carnival ride tickets cost 10 for $12.50. Which would be a reasonable cost for 25 tickets?

- ○ $20.00
- ○ $30.00
- ○ $40.00
- ○ none of the above

You have one die with the numbers 1, 2, 3, 4, 5, and 6. Expressed as a fraction, what is the probability of rolling a 2 if you roll 5 times? _____

Assessment

1

572
x 223

2

25)557

3 At the video arcade, Ely can play 8 games for $3.00. Which would be a reasonable cost of 20 games?

○ $7.00   ○ $10.00
○ $15.00   ○ $20.00

4 Gillian bought 48 hair scrunchies on sale for $10.00. She wants to keep 6 for herself and give the rest to 7 of her friends. If she shares the scrunchies equally, how many will she give to each friend? _____

5 (4 x 3) + (4 x 7) is equivalent to

○ (4 + 7) x 7

○ (4 + 4) x (7 x 7)

○ 4 x (7 + 3)

○ (4 x 3) – 7

○ none of the above

6 List the jobs in Norway from least to greatest number of workers.

1. _____
2. _____
3. _____
4. _____
5. _____
6. _____

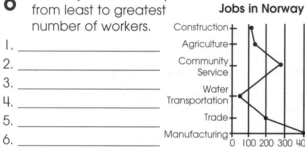

Jobs in Norway

7 Which number has a 9 in the hundred billions place?

○ 392,107,456,025

○ 189,502,011,047

○ 907,356

○ 961,077,684

8 Which are corresponding angles?

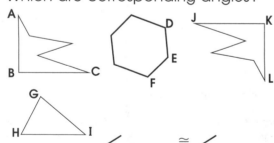

∠ _____ ≅ ∠ _____

9 Tito is buying 7 miniature model sets. Each set costs $4.89 including tax. How much change will Tito receive if he gives the clerk $40.00? _____

10 Inez has a packet of stationery with 42 sheets of colored paper. She used 14 sheets to write letters to her pen pals. What is the fraction for the portion of sheets she used?

○ $\frac{1}{2}$ ○ $\frac{1}{3}$ ○ $\frac{2}{7}$ ○ $\frac{4}{6}$

Write in expanded form.

2,310,107,900 _____
_____
_____

125,320,900 _____
_____
_____

Match.

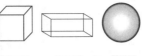

_____   _____   _____

_____   _____   _____

A. cone   C. cylinder
B. sphere   D. cube
E. triangular prism
F. rectangular prism

Two hundred forty fifth-graders were going on a field trip. Eighty students can ride on each bus. How many buses will be needed for the field trip? _____

209
x 634

572
x 468

Find a common denominator for the fraction. Shade in each figure to show the new fractions. Add to find the sum.

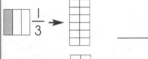 $\frac{1}{3}$ → _____

 $\frac{2}{4}$ → + _____

= _____

Which number should replace the **?** in each equation?

$(4.7 + 3.8) + 1.2 = 4.7 + (3.8 + ?)$

? = _____

$8.2 + (0.71 + 9.36) = (8.2 + ?) + 9.36$

? = _____

Mrs. Yates bought 5 cans of asparagus spears that were on special at 10 for $8.00. She gave the clerk a $10 bill. How much change will she receive?

_____

Font Town's community growth plan is illustrated in the above picture. If the town adds a new building and a new tree every two years, how many will Font Town have in ten years? _____ buildings
_____ trees

Continue counting. Write the next five numbers.
2,895,600
2,896,600
2,897,600
2,898,600

_____
_____
_____
_____
_____

If the perimeter of this fenced garden is 339 feet, what is the length of the missing side?

____ feet

62 ft.   58 ft.
?
39 ft.   71 ft.
39 ft.   45 ft.

B
25   26   27

Point B best represents which number?

○ 25.029
○ 25.321
○ 25.628
○ 25.989
○ none of the above

---

26)988

87)423

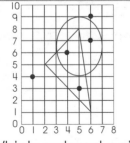

Which ordered pair is inside both the triangle and the circle? _____

Fat Max, the cat, is twice as fat as Garfield. Tubby Tabby is almost as big as Fat Max. Skinny Scat is thinner than Garfield but fatter than Bones. Use the back of this paper and write conclusions to compare:
1. Tubby Tabby to Garfield
2. Garfield to Fat Max
3. Bones to Garfield
4. Skinny Scat to Tubby Tabby

The Ford Family attended World on Parade. Each of the 8 exhibits they saw cost between $5.00 and $12.00 per family. What is a reasonable total spent by the Fords on visiting the exhibits?

○ $39.00
○ $79.00
○ $119.00
○ none of the above

You have one die with the numbers 1, 2, 3, 4, 5, and 6. Expressed as a fraction, what is the probability of rolling a double (2 of the same number) in 25 rolls? _____

Assessment

1

807
x 543

2

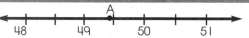

48)954

3 ▼ ❑ ■ ✳ ● ○

Mary is creating a design using the above shapes. Every 3 minutes, she adds another ▼ and another ❑. How many ▼ and ❑ will be in her design after 30 minutes? _____

4

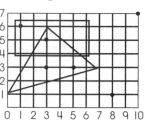

Which number does Point A best represent?

○ 49.457

○ 49.124

○ 49.589

○ 49.970

5 An old-fashioned steam train conducts scenic mountain tours. Each train car can hold 76 passengers. How many train cars are needed for a tour of 912 people?

_____

6 Which ordered pair is inside the rectangle and the triangle? _____

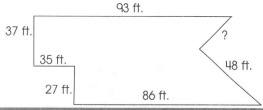

7 Natika bought 8 folders that were on sale for 12 for $4.68. She gave the clerk $10.00. How much change should she receive? _____

8 The perimeter of this shape is 349 feet. What is the length of the missing side? _____ feet

93 ft.

37 ft.

?

35 ft.

48 ft.

27 ft.

86 ft.

9

$\frac{1}{4}$ ⟶ ⟶ _____

+ $\frac{2}{5}$ ⟶ ⟶ + _____

= _____

10 Mr. Talbot bought 7 items at the discount store. Each item cost between $6.00 and $15.00. What is a reasonable total cost of Mr. Talbot's items?

○ $14.00

○ $54.00

○ $74.00

○ $124.00

○ none of the above

Day #1

Write in expanded form.

27,504,821 _____
_____
_____

65,457 _____
_____

Which figures have only one line of symmetry?

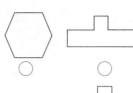

On a business trip in Canada, Mr. Yuma stopped several times to buy gas. His car needed 12.4 liters when he filled up the first time. At his next gas stop, his car needed 22.8 liters. The last time he stopped for gas, the car needed 18.6 liters. How many liters of gas did his car use on the trip? _____

3.9
x 7

7.5
x 9

Day #2

The above models show

○ $\frac{3}{6} > \frac{1}{2}$

○ $\frac{3}{6} < \frac{1}{2}$

○ $\frac{3}{6} = \frac{1}{2}$

$6^2 =$

○ 6 + 6
○ 6 x 6
○ 6 ÷ 6

$3^3 =$

○ 3 + 3
○ 3 + 3 + 3
○ 3 x 3 x 3

---

7 hours 34 minutes
– 2 hours 56 minutes

5 hours 10 minutes
– 3 hours 25 minutes

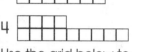

Use the grid below to shade in the 7th pattern

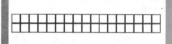

Day #3

Continue counting. Write the next six numbers.
5,682,301
5,782,301
5,882,301
5,982,301
_____
_____
_____
_____
_____
_____

The area of this rectangular swimming pool is 84 square feet. What is the length of the missing side? _____ feet

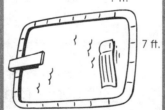

? ft.

7 ft.

Nine hundred twenty-seven thousand, four hundred and sixty-two thousandths is written

○ 927.462
○ 9,270.62
○ 9027,400.6
○ 9,400,274.0062
○ none of the above

8⟌72.80

5⟌45.35

Day #4

Which ordered pairs are outside both the triangle and the square? _____

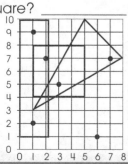

Bossy Boots bossed around an average of 35 people during the school week. On Monday she bossed around 7 people, on Wednesday she bossed around 6 people, on Thursday she bossed around 4 people, and on Friday she bossed around 8 people. How many people did she boss around on Tuesday?

_____

The Chicago O'Hare Airport has an average of 900,279 aircraft take-offs and landings per year. About how many aircraft take off or land at O'Hare each hour?

○ 105
○ 1,050
○ 10,500
○ not here

Hair Colors in Mr. Brock's Class

blonde	卌 lll
brown	卌 卌
red	lll
black	卌 lll

If one student was selected at random from Mr. Brock's class, what is the probability that the student would have blonde hair?

_____ out of _____

Assessment

1

$$\begin{array}{r} 4.7 \\ \times\ 7 \\ \hline \end{array}$$

2

$6\overline{)48.42}$

3 In 1980, the volcanic crater of Mt. St. Helens enlarged 1,450 feet in 13 days due to the magma pressure. About how many feet did the crater enlarge per day?

- ○ 100 ft.
- ○ 200 ft.
- ○ 300 ft.
- ○ 400 ft.

4 Mr. Harp put 6.8 liters of cleaner in his pool on Monday. On Friday, he added 4.6 more liters of cleaner. On the following Monday, 8.9 liters of cleaner was needed. How many liters of cleaner did Mr. Harp put in his pool? _____

5 $9^2 =$
- ○ $9 + 9$
- ○ 9×2
- ○ 9×9

$7^5 =$
- ○ $7 + 7 + 7 + 7 + 7$
- ○ 7×5
- ○ $7 \times 7 \times 7 \times 7 \times 7$

6 Continue counting. Write the next seven numbers.

23,597,123 _____
23,697,123 _____
23,797,123 _____
23,897,123 _____
_____
_____
_____

7 Write in expanded form.

89,403,276 _____
_____
_____

45,210 _____
_____
_____

8 Which figures have only one line of symmetry?

   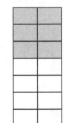

○   ○   ○   ○

9
$$\begin{array}{r} 8 \text{ hours } 21 \text{ minutes} \\ -\ 3 \text{ hours } 47 \text{ minutes} \\ \hline \end{array}$$

$$\begin{array}{r} 5 \text{ hours } 53 \text{ minutes} \\ -\ 1 \text{ hour } 17 \text{ minutes} \\ \hline \end{array}$$

10 Which fractions do the models show?

- ○ $\frac{1}{6} > \frac{5}{12}$
- ○ $\frac{1}{6} < \frac{5}{12}$
- ○ $\frac{1}{6} = \frac{5}{12}$

- ○ $\frac{4}{7} > \frac{6}{14}$
- ○ $\frac{4}{7} < \frac{6}{14}$
- ○ $\frac{4}{7} = \frac{6}{14}$

Steffi was reading about the Jurassic period of prehistoric life. The number she read about had an 8 in the ten millions place, and a 1 in the hundred millions place. Steffi found out that the Jurassic period began _____ years ago.

Match.
A. parallelogram
B. trapezoid
C. pentagon
D. quadrilateral
E. rhombus
F. octagon

At Disney World, Nigel wanted to buy souvenirs for himself and his friends. He bought 2 caps for $8.00 each, 5 sets of Disney stamps for $6.00 a set, and 3 banners for $7.50. How much did Nigel spend on souvenirs? _____

$$\begin{array}{r} 27.093 \\ \times \quad 25 \\ \hline \end{array}$$

$$\begin{array}{r} 13.521 \\ \times \quad 22 \\ \hline \end{array}$$

 This model shows $\frac{1}{6}$ shaded. **X** the model below that also shows $\frac{1}{6}$ shaded.

$7^2 =$ _____

$5^3 =$ _____

$2^{10} =$ _____

$10^2 =$ _____

$$\begin{array}{l} 8 \text{ hours } 54 \text{ minutes} \\ + 6 \text{ hours } 28 \text{ minutes} \\ \hline \end{array}$$

$$\begin{array}{l} 12 \text{ hours } 47 \text{ minutes} \\ + 13 \text{ hours } 38 \text{ minutes} \\ \hline \end{array}$$

Use the blank grid to shade in the 10th pattern.

Write this group of numbers in order from least to greatest.

12,645.79   12,645.97

126,425.1   6,654.99

1,264,500.07

1. _____
2. _____
3. _____
4. _____
5. _____

Find the volume of this box.

_____ cubic cm

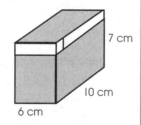

7 cm

10 cm

6 cm

Forty-one billion, two hundred million, sixty-three thousand, eight hundred and nine thousandths is written

○ 41,200,063,800.009

○ 4,200,630,008.9

○ 412,063,080.90

○ 410,263,809,800.09

○ none of the above

$6\overline{)48.84}$

$9\overline{)720.36}$

Magazine Sales

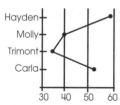

Hayden
Molly
Trimont
Carla

30   40   50   60

Circle the graph to the right that best matches the data shown on the above graph.

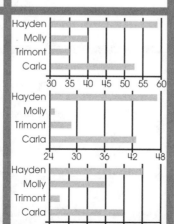

Light travels in a vacuum at the speed of 186,282 miles per second. Which is the best estimate of how fast light travels per minute?
(mpm = miles per minute)

○ 1,000 mpm

○ 3,000 mpm

○ 5,000 mpm

○ 10,000 mpm

○ not here

Ms. Lee's Class's Favorite Sports

baseball	ЖЖ ЖЖ		
soccer	ЖЖ ЖЖ			
tennis				
swimming	ЖЖ		

If one student was selected at random from Ms. Lee's class, what is the probability that the student's favorite sport would be either tennis or soccer? ____ out of ____

Assessment

1

$$34,021 \times 55$$

2

$$8 \overline{)64.56}$$

3

Mr. Todd's Class's Favorite Movies	
The Incredibles	卌 卌 卌
Spider Man 2	卌 卌
Toy Story 2	|||
Finding Nemo	卌 ||||

The probability of a randomly selected student in Mr. Todd's class choosing the movie *Finding Nemo* is _____ out of _____.

4 Fifty-nine billion, three hundred seventy-six million, two hundred eight thousand, and one thousandth is written

○ 59,376,208.1

○ 59,376,208,000.001

○ 593,762,008.100

○ 590,376,208.01

5 Holly was redecorating her room. She bought 3 sets of curtains for $13.98 a set, 4 throw pillows for $8.25 each, and 2 posters for $5.00 a piece. How much did Holly spend on redecorating her room? _____

6

Naper Family Vacation Journal Entries

Circle the graph to the right that best matches the above graph.

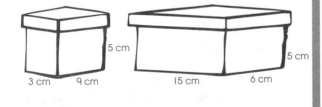

7

$$9 \text{ hours } 35 \text{ minutes} + 3 \text{ hours } 49 \text{ minutes}$$

$$15 \text{ hours } 28 \text{ minutes} + 23 \text{ hours } 59 \text{ minutes}$$

8 Find the volume of each box.

5 cm

3 cm   9 cm

5 cm

15 cm   6 cm

_____   _____

9 Henry's science project included riddles about space. One riddle said, "The approximate distance in light years that the Andromeda Galaxy is from Earth is a number that has a 2 in the hundred thousands place, and a 2 in the millions place." The Andromeda Galaxy is _____ light years from Earth.

10 The Pacific is the largest and deepest ocean. Its deepest point is the Mariana Trench, which is 36,198 feet below the surface. What is the best estimate of this depth in inches?

○ 100,00 inches

○ 200,00 inches

○ 300,000 inches

○ 400,000 inches

○ none of the above

Day #1

To which place have the pairs of numbers been rounded?

1,256 ⟶ 1,300

_____ place

27,230 ⟶ 30,000

_____ place

Circle the pairs of figures that are NOT congruent.

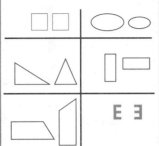

A delivery truck is hauling 7 crates of boxed stereo speakers. Each box contains 12 speakers and each crate contains 8 boxes. How many stereo speakers is the delivery truck hauling? _____

31.222
x   0.11

18.007
x   0.42

Day #2

Add and simplify the fractions.

$\frac{1}{2} + \frac{2}{5} =$ ____

$\frac{2}{8} + \frac{2}{32} =$ ____

$\frac{4}{9} - \frac{1}{6} =$ ____

$\frac{5}{7} - \frac{3}{5} =$ ____

If 7 times a number is 84, which equation could be used to find the number?

○ 84 x 7 = n

○ 84 ÷ 7 = n

○ 84 + 7 = n

○ 84 − 7 = n

---

sunscreen	2 for $1.40
shampoo	4 for $4.00
insect candles	6 for $16.00

The items above are sold only in multiples of 2, 4, or 6. Stacy wants to buy an equal number of items to take with her to camp. What is the least number of each she can buy, and how much will she spend? _____

Row 1

Row 2

Can you find and describe 3 patterns in the above figures?

_____

_____

_____

Day #3

Write this group of numbers in order from greatest to least.

254,005.092
2,545.2
2,545.002
25,405.01
254,000.97

1. _____
2. _____
3. _____
4. _____
5. _____

Find the missing dimension.

The volume is 90 cubic cm.

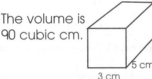

5 cm
3 cm

The volume is 100 cubic cm.

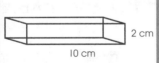

2 cm
10 cm

A   B   C
7   8   9

Write which point best represents

$\frac{65}{7}$ _____

$\frac{39}{5}$ _____

$\frac{68}{8}$ _____

---

9)1.026

12)25.08

Day #4

Go-Cart Time Trials MPH

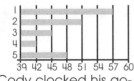

39 42 45 48 51 54 57 60

Cody clocked his go-cart five times and graphed the speeds in miles per hour. What is the average of his three best time trials?

_____ mph

Devon planted pumpkin vines. He noticed that for every 5 inches the vine grew, it also grew 3 new leaves. If the vine grows $2\frac{1}{2}$ inches every three days, how many leaves will the pumpkin vine have in 30 days? _____

Ken found that the Sears Tower has 110 stories and is 1,454 feet tall. He used his calculator to find the height of each story, which was 13.218181818 feet. Rounded to the nearest hundredth, how tall is each story in the Sears Tower?

_____ feet

Wes wanted to find out the probability of tossing a dime and a penny and having them both land on heads. He made a chart of the possible outcomes.

Dime	Penny	Outcomes
heads	tails	= HT
	heads	= HH
tails	tails	= TT
	heads	= TH

Expressed as a fraction, what is the probability of tossing 2 heads? _____

Assessment

1

$$55.204$$
$$\times \quad 0.22$$

2

$$7\overline{)1.89}$$

3 Simeon wanted to find the tax on a $23.00 remote control car. He multiplied the cost by the tax rate of 0.08236 and found that the tax would be $1.89428. Rounded to the nearest tenth, how much tax will Simeon pay? _____

4 In Bessie's Gift Shop, the clerk is arranging shadow boxes on wall shelves. There are 6 wall shelf units with 9 shelves per unit. If the clerk places 15 shadow boxes on each shelf, how many shadow boxes will be on display in the gift shop?

_____

5 If 9 times a number is 126. Which equation can be used to find the number *n*?

○ $126 + 9 = n$

○ $126 - 9 = n$

○ $126 \times 9 = n$

○ $126 \div 9 = n$

6 Write this group of numbers in order from greatest to least.

7,845.639

17,845.69

71,485.063

7,845.6

71,485.603

_____

_____

_____

_____

_____

7 To which place have the pairs of numbers been rounded?

$6,725 \longrightarrow 7,000$

_____ place

$92,345 \longrightarrow 92,350$

_____ place

8 Circle the pairs of figures that are NOT congruent.

9

air mattress	3 for $12.00
waterproof matches	12 boxes for $7.20
5 gal. propane bottles	2 for $7.00

Julio wants to purchase an equal number of each item above to take on a three-week hiking trip. The items are sold only in multiples of 2, 3, and 12. What is the least number he can purchase of each and how much will he spend? _____

10 Add or subtract and simplify if needed.

$$\frac{2}{5} + \frac{5}{6} = \underline{\quad}$$

$$\frac{1}{3} + \frac{8}{9} = \underline{\quad}$$

$$\frac{4}{9} - \frac{1}{3} = \underline{\quad}$$

To which place have the pairs of numbers been rounded?

26.429 → 26.430

_____

41.623 → 42.0

_____

Label F for flip and T for turn.

____ . ____

____

B B

____

A craft store received 12 cartons of ribbon. There are 25 spools of ribbon in each carton, and each spool holds 329 inches of ribbon. How many inches of ribbon are contained in each carton? _____

$$4.18$$
$$\times\ 2.32$$

$$0.705$$
$$\times\ 1.20$$

Add or subtract. Simplify the fractions.

$2\frac{1}{8} + 5\frac{1}{3} =$ _____

$5\frac{2}{3} - 2\frac{2}{9} =$ _____

$2\frac{1}{4} + 5\frac{9}{10} =$ _____

$7\frac{1}{8} - 5\frac{5}{12} =$ _____

Complete the equations.

$(9 \times 8) \div 6 = 3 \times \boxed{}$

$3 \times \boxed{} = 4 \times \boxed{}$

$100 - 75 = 5 \times \boxed{}$

---

soda	18 for $12.00
plastic cups	9 for $2.00
chips	3 bags for $3.00

Mrs. MacLaren wants to buy an equal number of the above items for the school picnic. The items are sold only in multiples of 3, 9, and 18. What is the least number of each she can purchase, and how much will she spend on the items? _____

_____

What is the rule?

$\frac{3}{6}$ ⟶ 1

$\frac{6}{18}$ ⟶ $\frac{15}{18}$

$\frac{1}{7}$ ⟶ $\frac{9}{14}$

$\frac{3}{5}$ ⟶ $1\frac{1}{10}$

_____

Write > or < to compare.

25.037 $\boxed{}$ 25.307

9,267.52 $\boxed{}$ 9,263.88

32,947.1 $\boxed{}$ 3,297.9

985.269 $\boxed{}$ 985.264

1,007.057 $\boxed{}$ 1,007.02

By using the line of symmetry, what is the length of line segment FG?_____

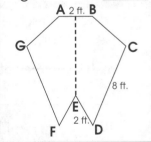

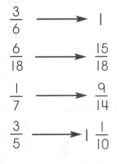

Which point best represents

$\frac{79}{7}$ _____

$\frac{121}{9}$ _____

$\frac{154}{12}$ _____

$39\overline{)163.8}$

$84\overline{)530.88}$

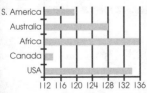

Highest Recorded Temperature (Degrees Fahrenheit)

The total degrees Fahrenheit for the 3 highest temperatures is _____ °F.

A garden maze is built in the shape of a hexagon inside an octagon. Each side, both inner and outer, have arching vines for doorways. Each arch is made of 12 gourd vines. How many gourd vines are in the maze? _____

Mr. Rodriguez travels from Boston to Salt Lake City, a distance of about 4,848.821 miles round trip. On average, he makes this trip 9.25 times a year. Rounded to the nearest tenth of a mile, how far does he travel each year? _____

A	B
1	1, 2, 3
2	1, 2, 3
3	1, 2, 3

What is the probability of spinning a 2 on both spinners?

1

$$139 \times .25$$

2

$$48\overline{)124.8}$$

3

$\frac{2}{6} \rightarrow 1$	$\frac{1}{2} \rightarrow 1\frac{1}{6}$
$\frac{4}{15} \rightarrow \frac{14}{15}$	$\frac{2}{7} \rightarrow \frac{20}{21}$

What is the rule? _____

4

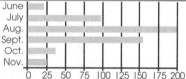

Which point best represents

$\frac{98}{15}$ ___ $\frac{43}{9}$ ___ $\frac{104}{20}$ ___ $\frac{65}{9}$ ___

5 Lotty's Fruit Drink Café ordered 27 cases of drink mixes. Each case holds 24 boxes, and each box contains 250 individual packets of fruit drink mix. How many individual packets of fruit drink mix are in each case? _____

6

The best estimate for the total number of hurricanes during the three highest frequency months is

○ 250   ○ 350
○ 450   ○ 550

7 Cobblestone walls surround an oriental garden built in the shape of a triangle. These walls are inside another square-shaped wall. From the outside going in there is a door on every wall. Each door has a 12-board slatted gate. How many boards are in the garden gates?

_____

8 Using the line of symmetry, what is the length of line segment AB? _____

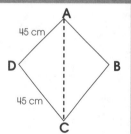

9 To which place have the numbers been rounded?

35.87 ⟶ 35.9

_____ place

10.621 ⟶ 11.0

_____ place

10 Mrs. Kline spends an average of $173.82 per week on groceries. Rounded to the nearest dollar, about how much does she spend each year?

(52 weeks = 1 year)

○ $9,040.64
○ $9,050.00
○ $9,039.00
○ $9,100.00
○ none of the above

Using the numbers 2–9 one time each in the patterns below, create the greatest and least number possible.

greatest

_ _ _ _ _ . _ _ _

least

_ _ _ _ _ . _ _ _

Label F for flip and T for turn.

___

___

___

Kim bought party favors. Underline the equation that shows how to find the total number of items she bought if she purchased 8 bags of 23 balloons, 7 packs of 12 party hats, and 15 packages of 4 gumballs.

○ $(8 + 23) \times (7 + 12) \times (15 + 4)$

○ $(8 \times 23) \times (7 \times 12) \times (15 \times 4)$

○ $(8 \times 23) + (7 \times 12) + (15 \times 4)$

$$\begin{array}{r} 12.52 \\ \times \quad 8.4 \\ \hline \end{array}$$

$$\begin{array}{r} 560.903 \\ + 429.598 \\ \hline \end{array}$$

A ratio is used to compare two quantities.

▲▲■■■■○
□□□□□□★

▲ compared to □ is 2 to 6.

Write the ratios for

★ to ■ _____

○ to ▲ _____

■ to □ _____

Prime numbers have only two factors. Composite numbers have more than two factors. Label each number below as P (prime) or C (composite).

12 _____   7 _____

33 _____   25 _____

5 _____   111 _____

An adult hippopotamus eats about 130 pounds of vegetable matter per day. How many pounds of vegetable matter would a hippopotamus eat during the month of July? _____

About how many tons of food would this be? _____

What is the rule?

_____

$\dfrac{6}{20} \longrightarrow \dfrac{2}{20}$

$\dfrac{2}{3} \longrightarrow \dfrac{7}{15}$

$\dfrac{1}{2} \longrightarrow \dfrac{3}{10}$

$\dfrac{7}{12} \longrightarrow \dfrac{23}{60}$

Write > or < to compare.

0.25×4 ☐ 0.012×12

$23.65 - 0.89$ ☐ $21.60 + 0.97$

$69.12 \div 3$ ☐ 23.91×0.2

0.45×0.45 ☐ $0.26 + 0.26$

For the 4th of July celebration the city used 3,500 meters of red, white, and blue crepe paper to decorate the park pavilion. How many kilometers of crepe paper did they use? ___

How many centimeters of crepe paper would this be? _____

Write the number for

twenty-seven billion, four hundred ninety-two million, eight

_____

six hundred fifty million, one hundred two thousand, five hundred

_____

$$97\overline{)340.664}$$

$$\begin{array}{r} 621.027 \\ - 518.634 \\ \hline \end{array}$$

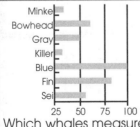

Minke
Bowhead
Gray
Killer
Blue
Fin
Sei

25   50   75   100

Which whales measure over 50 feet in length?

_____

_____

_____

A medieval castle's first story is in the shape of an octagon, the second story is in the shape of a hexagon, and the third story is in the shape of a square. On each level, each corner has a merlon with 8 openings where the castle's defenders could set their weapons. How many such openings are in this castle? _____

A   **B**

If basket A can hold 125 apples, about how many of basket B would be needed to fill basket A?

○ 1

○ 2

○ 10

○ 20

$1\dfrac{1}{4} + 2\dfrac{3}{4} =$ _____

$7\dfrac{2}{3} + 3\dfrac{8}{9} =$ _____

$9\dfrac{1}{3} - 2\dfrac{2}{3} =$ _____

$6 - 1\dfrac{4}{12} =$ _____

Assessment

1

$$10.5 \times 9.37$$

$$\frac{6}{9}$$
$$\frac{5}{7}$$
$$+ \overline{}$$

2

$$13\overline{)377.65}$$

3
If bag A can hold 215 marbles, how many of bag B would it take to fill bag A?

○ $1\frac{1}{2}$ ○ 3   ○ $5\frac{1}{2}$

4 For the PTA banquet, Ms. Kim bought 8 cases of 12-pack sodas, 15 cartons of 10-pack juice drinks, and 4 boxes of 4-can juice concentrate. Which equation shows how to find the total number of drinks she bought?

○ (8 x 12) + (15 x 10) + (4 x 4)

○ (8 + 12) + (15 + 10) + (4 + 4)

○ 8 x (12 + 15) x 10 + (4 x 4)

5 Prime numbers have only two factors. Composite numbers have more than two factors. Label each numeral below as P (prime) or C (composite).

36 _____   9 _____

73 _____   67 _____

13 _____   204 _____

6 Write > or < to compare.

0.35 x 8 ☐ 5.23 + 0.078

82.061 – 74.359 ☐ 49.49 ÷ 7

0.962 x 0.53 ☐ 0.978 x 0.67

7 Using the numbers 0, 2, 4, 6, 8, 9, 7, 5 one time each in the patterns below, create the greatest and least number possible.

greatest

__ __ __ __ __ . __ __ __

least

__ __ __ __ __ . __ __ __

8 Label F for flip and T for turn.

_____   _____   _____

9 Camels that graze in the Sahara may go all winter without water, but in the summer they may drink 19 liters of water a day. How many liters of water might a camel drink during 3 weeks in the summer? _____

10 The ratio of 🐑 to 🐑 is 7:1.

What is the ratio of

 to _____

 to  _____

0-7682-3205-8 *Math 4 Today*

Day #1

Which number has a digit of lesser value in the hundred thousands place than in the hundreds place?

- ○ 75,462,190
- ○ 369,502,431
- ○ 2,156,287,302
- ○ 8,032,265,299

Give the number of vertices, faces, and edges.

V	F	E

Dennis bought 15 stamp albums for $1.35 each and 4 baseball card sets for $6.89 a piece. Eric bought 6 comic books for $2.45 each, and 7 packs of model seals for $4.76 each. What is the difference in the amount of change due the boys if they both gave the cashier $50.00? _____
_____

```
   45.521
 1,259.000
  786.099
+57,877.020
_____


  78,866.039
− 31,427.060
_____
```

Day #2

Equivalent fractions name equal ratios. For example: 2:3 or $\frac{2}{3}$ is the same as 4:6 or $\frac{4}{6}$.

List at least two other equal ratios for 2:3.

_____ _____

Complete the factor tree to find the prime factorization.

```
      12
      2 x 6
prime→ 2 x 2 x 3
factors

      40
      10 x 4
__ x __ x __ x __
```

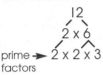
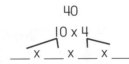

A hummingbird's wings beat about 68.9 times a second. How many beats is this per hour? _____

About how many beats would this be per day?

_____

Continue the pattern. Write the next five numbers.
24.859
24.874
24.889
24.904
_____
_____
_____
_____
_____

Day #3

Planets	Equatorial Diameter in Kilometers
Saturn	120,660
Earth	12,756
Uranus	51,810
Jupiter	142,800
Neptune	49,528

List the planets in order from least to greatest diameter.
1. _____
2. _____
3. _____
4. _____
5. _____

The highway department painted a new stripe on $7\frac{1}{2}$ kilometers of highway. The paint truck carried enough paint for 500 meters. How many times did the truck need to refill to paint the new stripe? _____
How many decameters long was the stripe? _____

Write the number for

six hundred seventy-one billion, five hundred three million, eighty-two thousand, thirty-four

_____

three billion, two hundred nine thousand, six hundred forty-seven

_____

To multiply fractions, multiply the numerators, then multiply the denominators.

$\frac{2}{3}$ x $\frac{2}{3}$ ⇉ $\frac{4}{9}$

$\frac{1}{7}$ x $\frac{6}{8}$ = ____

$\frac{4}{5}$ x $\frac{6}{10}$ = ____

$\frac{3}{8}$ x $\frac{5}{7}$ = ____

Day #4

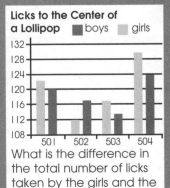

Licks to the Center of a Lollipop ■ boys ■ girls

What is the difference in the total number of licks taken by the girls and the total number of licks taken by the boys? _____

The seven dwarfs measured their heights. Sleepy is taller than Grumpy. Dopey is taller than Sneezy. Doc is not as a tall as Sneezy. Bashful is taller than Grumpy but not as tall as Sleepy. Happy is shorter than Doc. Which dwarf is the tallest? _____

the shortest? _____

in the middle? _____

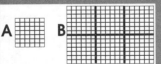

A   B

If page A holds 362 stamps, about how many stamps would be needed to fill page B?
- ○ 500
- ○ 1,000
- ○ 1,500
- ○ 2,000

$8 - 5\frac{6}{10}$ = ____

$3\frac{7}{20} - 1\frac{2}{5}$ = ____

$9\frac{10}{16} + 3\frac{7}{8}$ = ____

$6\frac{11}{15} + 5\frac{4}{5}$ = ____

Assessment

1

```
      0.057
  2,188.800
    792.396
+ 45,237.000
```

$$\frac{4}{18}$$
$$\frac{6}{12}$$
$$+ \phantom{\frac{6}{12}}$$

2

$$\frac{3}{10} \times \frac{7}{8} = \underline{\hspace{1cm}}$$

$$\frac{9}{12} \times \frac{5}{7} = \underline{\hspace{1cm}}$$

3 Continue the pattern. Write the next four numbers

39.452 _____

39.562 _____

39.672 _____

39.782 _____

4 Write the number for

fifty-one million, nine hundred seventy-eight thousand, four hundred

_____

sixty billion, twenty-five million, three hundred six thousand, eighteen

_____

5 Trenda bought 5 sets of deco-nails for $3.50 a set and 12 hair clips for $2.00 a piece. Lisha bought 8 bangle bracelets for $2.34 each and 4 pairs of earrings for $5.00 a pair. What is the difference in the amount of change due the girls if they both give the cashier $50.00? _____

_____

6 Clyde and Clem competed in the annual Seed Spittin' Contest. Who won? _____

By how many inches did this person win? _____

Watermelon Seed Spittin' Contest

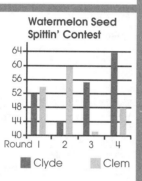

Round 1 2 3 4

■ Clyde   ■ Clem

7 The Lazies got tired of yawning and began arguing about who is the laziest person in the family. Shut-eye is lazier than Lulu but not as lazy as Tuckered. Snoozy is lazier than Slug but not as lazy as Sleepy. Slug is almost as lazy as Tuckered. Who is the laziest? _____

8 Mr. Hernandez is rebuilding the fence around his grazing pasture. The perimeter of the pasture is 8 kilometers. His pickup can haul enough lumber for fencing 250 meters at a time. How many loads of lumber will he need to haul to complete the fence? _____

9 Which number has a digit of lesser value in the hundred thousands place than in the billions place?

○ 124,560,738,016

○ 3,689,920,315

○ 78,565,830,716

○ 342,189,375,002

○ none of the above

10 Complete the factor trees.

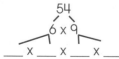

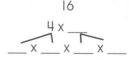

Day #1

Name the place and the value of the 9 in each number.

79,462,150 _____

_____

3,872,109 _____

_____

2,159,476 _____

_____

Give the number of vertices, faces, and edges.

V	F	E

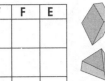

Yesenia needed to do an 840-word research paper for science. After typing 3 pages of her report, she had her computer do a line count. Each page had 15 lines with an average of 14 words per line. How many pages does she still need to type. _____

$6\frac{3}{8}$

$2\frac{1}{4}$

$+\ 7\frac{9}{16}$

$12\frac{5}{7}$

$8\frac{2}{3}$

$+\ \frac{}{}$

$13\frac{1}{4}$

$-\ 4\frac{2}{3}$

Day #2

Molly needs 2 teaspoons of cooking oil to make 6 fudge cakes. Complete the ratio chart to see how much cooking oil is needed to make other quantities of fudge cakes?

teaspoons of oil

	2					
3	6	18	30	54	100	

fudge cakes

Complete the factor trees to find the prime factorization.

63

____ x ____ x ____ prime factors

44

____ x ____ x ____ prime factors

Tinker's Toy Store Sale

Item	Regular Price	Sale Price
football	$4.89	$3.99
water gun	$32.15	$29.79
model	$7.49	$5.19

How much money can Ted save by buying 2 footballs, 1 water gun, and 3 models at the sale prices?

_____

If this pattern continues, what will the center row look like?

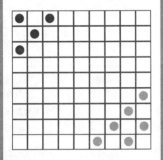

Day #3

Kilometer, meter, inch, foot, mile, yard, centimeter, and millimeter. List the units of standard and metric measure in order from least to greatest.

1. _____ 5. _____
2. _____ 6. _____
3. _____ 7. _____
4. _____ 8. _____

In Jules Verne's *Twenty Thousand Leagues Under the Sea*, Captain Nemo takes a submarine voyage. A nautical league equals 5.556 kilometers or about 3.452 miles. How many kilometers deep did Captain Nemo's sub descend? _____

How many miles? ____

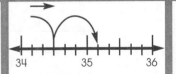

This number line shows

○ $34 + 1\frac{1}{2} = 35\frac{1}{2}$

○ $34\frac{1}{2} + \frac{2}{3} = 35\frac{1}{6}$

○ $34\frac{3}{4} + 1 = 35\frac{3}{4}$

Multiply. Write the product in simplest terms.

$\frac{9}{15} \times \frac{3}{10} =$ ____

$\frac{3}{8} \times \frac{4}{5} =$ ____

$\frac{6}{30} \times \frac{2}{100} =$ ____

Day #4

Active Volcanic Sites

Indonesia 130
Philippines 100
Iceland 25
Japan 33
Chile 25

Of the active volcanic sites shown, Indonesia and the Philippines have

○ less than one-half
○ more than one-half
○ about one-third

Animal Speeds	Miles per Hour
cheetah	70
elk	45
zebra	40
rabbit	35
black mamba snake	20
chicken	9

The answer is "5 times as fast." What is the question?

_____

_____

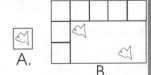

A.   B.

If aquarium A holds 57 fish, about how many fish would aquarium B hold?

○ 700   ○ 1,500

○ 900   ○ 2,000

If these cards are shuffled and placed facedown, what is the probability of drawing a

	in 1 draw	in 60 draws
☆		
✗		
◆		

Assessment

1

$$5\frac{5}{8} \qquad 23\frac{9}{12} \qquad 10\frac{1}{5}$$
$$3\frac{7}{16} \qquad +\ 5\frac{6}{8} \qquad -\ 3\frac{3}{4}$$
$$+\ 4\frac{3}{4}$$

2

$$\frac{4}{32} \times \frac{1}{2} = \underline{\quad}$$

$$\frac{2}{9} \times \frac{4}{6} = \underline{\quad}$$

3

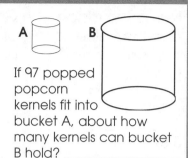

If 97 popped popcorn kernels fit into bucket A, about how many kernels can bucket B hold? _____

4 Élan is collecting baseball cards. His goal is to collect 2,000 cards. He already has 3 baseball card albums. Each album has 24 pages and each page holds 16 cards. Show how to find out how many more baseball cards Élan needs to meet his goal.

_____

5 Complete the factor tree.

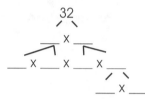

6 List the units of standard and metric measure in order from greatest to least.

meter	inch
kilometer	mile
centimeter	foot
millimeter	yard

_____
_____
_____
_____
_____
_____

7 Name the place and the value of the 5 in each number.

52,178,096 _____
_____

8,523,746 _____
_____

340,096.852 _____
_____

8 Give the number of vertices, faces, and edges for each figure.

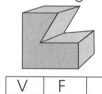

V	F	E

V	F	E

9

Martin's Music and More Sale

Item	Regular Price	Sale Price
cassettes	$6.73	$4.97
blank videos	$8.29	$7.79
select CDs	$13.88	$11.99

How much money can be saved by buying 3 cassettes, 2 blank videos, and 1 CD at the sale prices? _____

10 The Old Steamers N' Gauge Model Train Club uses 15 sections of track to complete three rail layouts. Complete the ratio chart to find how much track is needed for other layouts.

sections of track
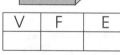

15				
1	3	9	15	50

rail layouts

Day #1

Name the place and the value of the 3 in each number.

1,372,650,919 _____

_____

3,107,254,041 _____

_____

9,876.532 _____

_____

Label each pair of figures S for similar or C for congruent.

____

____

____

The fireworks supply house delivered 856 sparklers, 494 bottle rockets, and 7 boxes of 125 Roman candles. Show how to find the number of firework assortment packages that can be made if 25 items are in each package. _____

$$4,325.672 + \boxed{}$$
$$\overline{5,010.649}$$

$8\frac{4}{5} + 3\frac{4}{6} = \boxed{}$

$15\frac{2}{9} - \frac{4}{6} = \boxed{}$

Day #2

Mr. Eugene makes 6 quarts of his special homemade ice cream by adding 4 eggs to his other secret ingredients. Complete the ratio chart to see how many eggs are needed for more ice cream.

eggs

	4				
3	6	18	30	120	$8\frac{1}{2}$

quarts of ice cream

Math Path

$462 \div 3 =$ _____ x 7

= _____ + 22 =

_____ ÷ 50 =

_____ − 2 = _____

Connie's Crafts

Item	Price
colored yarn	$5.00
glass beads	$3.00
picture frame	$7.50

Mrs. Wells purchased some items and received $1.50 in change from a $20.00 bill. What did Mrs. Wells buy? _____

_____

_____

What is the pattern? _____

Which row, if any, will be blank? _____

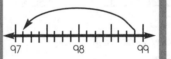

Day #3

Circle the larger unit of measure in each pair. If they are equal, circle both.

5 dm   1 m

500 mm   5 cm

100 m   1 km

100 cm   1 m

2,000 g   1 kg

Measuring Circles

π = pi = 3.14

circumference = *diameter x π*

area = *π x radius²*

Find the circumference and the area of the circle below.

12 mm

circumference = _____ mm

area = _____ mm²

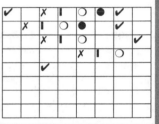

97   98   99

This number line shows

○ $97 + 1\frac{1}{2} = 98\frac{1}{2}$

○ $99\frac{1}{2} - \frac{5}{8} = 98\frac{1}{8}$

○ $98\frac{7}{8} - 1\frac{3}{4} = 97\frac{1}{8}$

$$7,150.034 - \boxed{}$$
$$\overline{1,048.379}$$

$$\boxed{}\,\overline{)22,308}\;\;^{572}$$

Day #4

U.S. Endangered Species

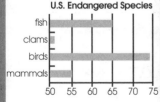

fish	
clams	
birds	
mammals	

50 55 60 65 70 75

The answer is "about 23." What is the question? _____

_____

_____

← continued

Answer: 139

Question? _____

_____

_____

Answer: 97

Question? _____

_____

_____

Tara completed 9 oil paintings. The shortest time she took to complete a painting was 3 weeks and the longest time she needed was 12 weeks. What is a reasonable estimate of the time it took to complete all 9 paintings?

○ 67 weeks

○ 114 weeks

○ 27 weeks

Complete the chart to show the probability of spinning a

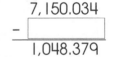

in 1 spin	in 40 spins
●	
○	
●	

Assessment

1

$$3,652.809$$
$$+ \boxed{}$$
$$\overline{5,003.475}$$

$$459$$
$$\times \boxed{}$$
$$\overline{37,179}$$

2

$$\boxed{}\,\overline{)17,296}^{\,368}$$

3 Complete the chart to show the probability of spinning

	in 1 spin	in 30 spins
🔵		
⚪		
⚫		

4

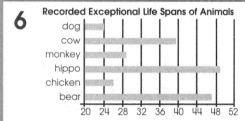

The number line shows

- ○ $54\frac{1}{8} - 1\frac{1}{2} = 52\frac{5}{8}$
- ○ $52 + 2 = 54$
- ○ $54\frac{2}{8} - 1\frac{1}{4} = 52\frac{1}{2}$
- ○ $54 - 2 = 52$

5 From a flood relief, Baker City received 309 dry goods, 452 drinks, and 36 cases of canned goods holding 124 cans each. Show how many food boxes the volunteers can pack so that each box has 55 items.

6 Recorded Exceptional Life Spans of Animals

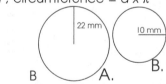

Write a question for each answer. Use the back of this paper to write.

1. about twice as many years as the dog
2. about 10 years longer

7 Susie's Sweet Shoppe

Item	Price
Gummi Yummies (bag)	$4.82
Chocolate Delights (box)	$10.33
Slurpy Sundae	$3.99

Pave and Margo bought some goodies at the Sweet Shoppe and received $1.87 change from $25.00. What did they buy?

_____

8 Find the area and circumference of each circle.

$\pi = 3.14$, area $= \pi\, r^2$, circumference $= d \times \pi$

22 mm   10 mm

A.   B.

Circle	A	B
Area	_____	_____
Circumference	_____	_____

9 Name the place and the value of the 2 in each number.

231,178,096   _____

          _____

3,029,541   _____

          _____

103,400.102   _____

          _____

10 Since their club began, the Quick Quilters have completed 13 quilts. The American Flag quilt took them 18 weeks to complete, which was their longest time. A baby quilt took them only 5 weeks to finish. What is a reasonable estimate of the time it took to complete all 13 quilts?

- ○ 15 weeks
- ○ 50 weeks
- ○ 150 weeks
- ○ 1,150 weeks
- ○ none of the above

Answer Key

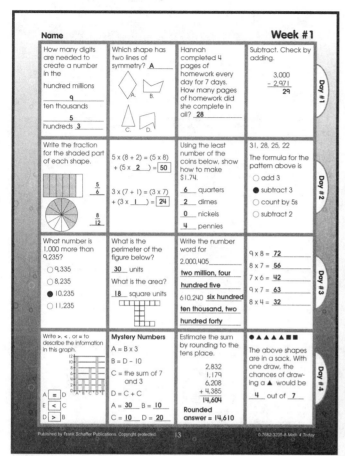

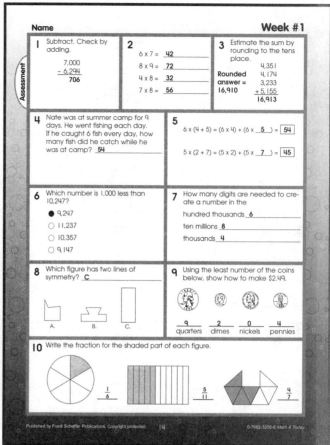

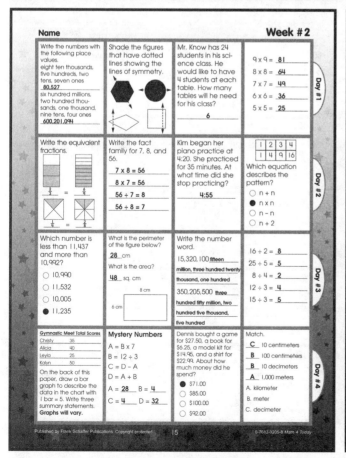

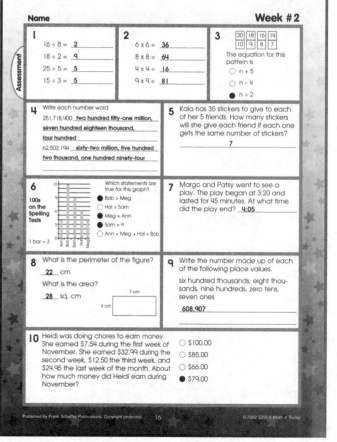

Answer Key

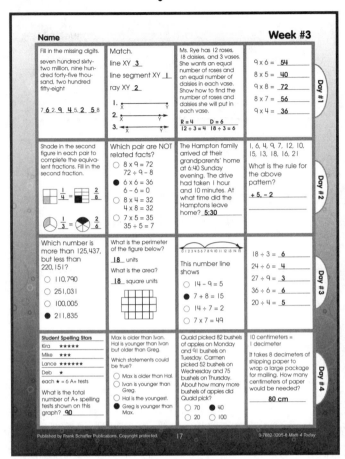

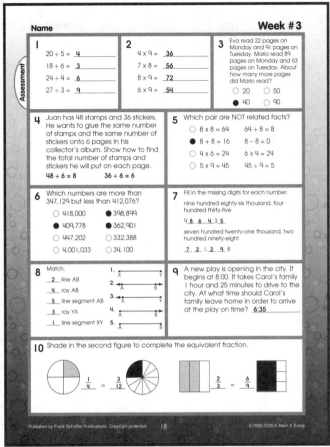

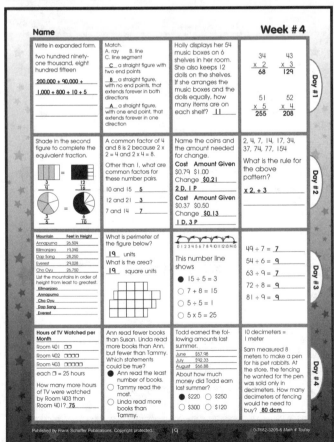

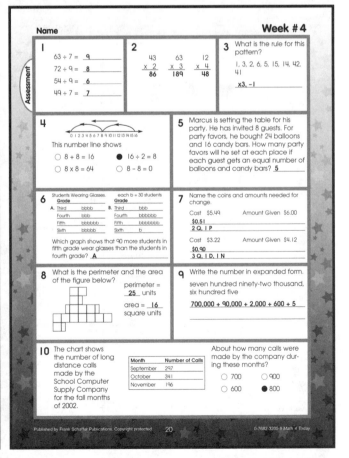

Answer Key

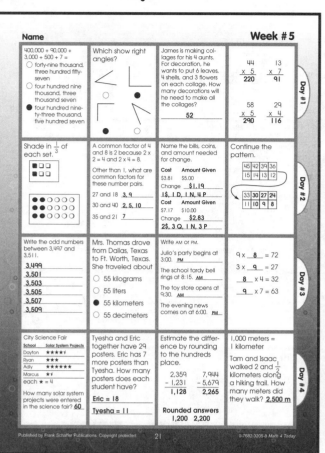

Name — Week # 5

Day #1

400,000 + 90,000 + 3,000 + 500 + 7 =
○ forty-nine thousand, three hundred fifty-seven
○ four hundred nine thousand, three thousand seven
● four hundred ninety-three thousand, five hundred seven

Which show right angles? (lower left filled, lower right open)

James is making collages for his 4 aunts. For decoration, he wants to put 6 leaves, 4 shells, and 3 flowers on each collage. How many decorations will he need to make all the collages? **52**

44 × 5 = 220   13 × 7 = 91
58 × 5 = 290   29 × 4 = 116

Day #2

Shade in ⅓ of each set.

A common factor of 4 and 8 is 2 because 2 × 2 = 4 and 2 × 4 = 8.
Other than 1, what are common factors for these number sets?
27 and 18 **3, 9**
30 and 40 **2, 5, 10**
35 and 21 **7**

Name the bills, coins, and amount needed for change.
Cost $3.81   Amount Given $5.00   Change **$1.19**   1$, 1 D, 1 N, 4 P
Cost $7.17   Amount Given $10.00   Change **$2.83**   2$, 3 Q, 1 N, 3 P

Continue the pattern.
45 42 39 36
15 14 13 12
33 30 27 24
11 10 9 8

Day #3

Write the odd numbers between 3,497 and 3,511.
3,499
3,501
3,503
3,505
3,507
3,509

Mrs. Thomas drove from Dallas, Texas to Ft. Worth, Texas. She traveled about
○ 55 kilograms
○ 55 liters
● 55 kilometers
○ 55 decimeters

Write AM or PM.
Julio's party begins at 3:00. **PM**
The school tardy bell rings at 8:15. **AM**
The toy store opens at 9:30. **AM**
The evening news comes on at 6:00. **PM**

9 × 8 = 72
3 × 9 = 27
8 × 4 = 32
9 × 7 = 63

Day #4

City Science Fair

School	Solar System Projects
Dayton	★★★★✦
Ryan	★★★
Adly	★★★★★★
Marcus	★✦

each ★ = 4
How many solar system projects were entered in the science fair? **60**

Tyesha and Eric together have 29 posters. Eric has 7 more posters than Tyesha. How many posters does each student have?
Eric = 18
Tyesha = 11

Estimate the difference by rounding to the hundreds place.
2,359 − 1,231 = 1,128
7,944 − 5,679 = 2,265
Rounded answers **1,200   2,200**

1,000 meters = 1 kilometer
Tam and Isaac walked 2½ kilometers along a hiking trail. How many meters did they walk? **2,500 m**

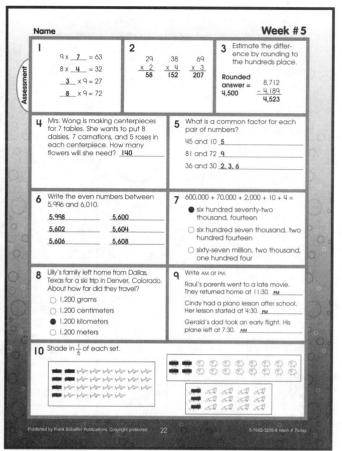

Name — Week # 5

Assessment

1
9 × **7** = 63
8 × **4** = 32
3 × 9 = 27
8 × 9 = 72

2
29 × 2 = 58
38 × 4 = 152
69 × 3 = 207

3 Estimate the difference by rounding to the hundreds place.
Rounded answer = 4,500
8,712 − 4,189 = 4,523

4 Mrs. Wong is making centerpieces for 7 tables. She wants to put 8 daisies, 7 carnations, and 5 roses in each centerpiece. How many flowers will she need? **140**

5 What is a common factor for each pair of numbers?
45 and 10 **5**
81 and 72 **9**
36 and 30 **2, 3, 6**

6 Write the even numbers between 5,996 and 6,010.
5,998   **5,600**
5,602   **5,604**
5,606   **5,608**

7 600,000 + 70,000 + 2,000 + 10 + 4 =
● six hundred seventy-two thousand, fourteen
○ six hundred seven thousand, two hundred fourteen
○ sixty-seven million, two thousand, one hundred four

8 Lilly's family left home from Dallas, Texas for a ski trip in Denver, Colorado. About how far did they travel?
○ 1,200 grams
○ 1,200 centimeters
● 1,200 kilometers
○ 1,200 meters

9 Write AM or PM.
Raul's parents went to a late movie. They returned home at 11:30. **PM**
Cindy had a piano lesson after school. Her lesson started at 4:30. **PM**
Gerald's dad took an early flight. His plane left at 7:30. **AM**

10 Shade in ⅕ of each set.

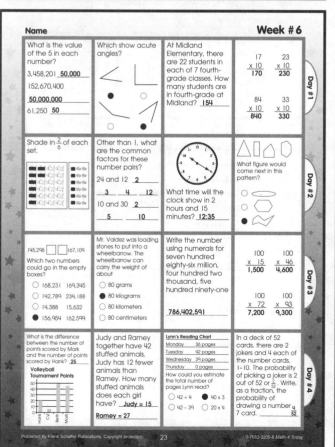

Name — Week # 6

Day #1

What is the value of the 5 in each number?
3,458,201 **50,000**
152,670,400 **50,000,000**
61,250 **50**

Which show acute angles? (upper right filled, lower left open)

At Midland Elementary, there are 22 students in each of 7 fourth-grade classes. How many students are in fourth-grade at Midland? **154**

17 × 10 = 170   23 × 10 = 230
84 × 10 = 840   33 × 10 = 330

Day #2

Shade in 2/6 of each set.

Other than 1, what are the common factors for these number pairs?
24 and 12 **2**
3   4   12
10 and 30 **2**
5

What time will the clock show in 2 hours and 15 minutes? **12:35**

What figure would come next in this pattern?
● (filled shape)

Day #3

145,298 ☐ ☐ 167,109
Which two numbers could go in the empty boxes?
○ 168,231   169,345
○ 142,789   234,188
○ 14,388   15,632
● 156,954   162,599

Mr. Valdez was loading stones to put into a wheelbarrow. The wheelbarrow can carry the weight of about
○ 80 grams
● 80 kilograms
○ 80 kilometers
○ 80 centimeters

Write the number using numerals for seven hundred eighty-six million, four hundred two thousand, five hundred ninety-one
786,402,591

100 × 15 = 1,500   100 × 46 = 4,600
100 × 72 = 7,200   100 × 93 = 9,300

Day #4

What is the difference between the number of points scored by Mark and the number of points scored by Hank? **25**
Volleyball Tournament Points (bar graph: Hank, Cyl, Beth, Mark)

Judy and Ramey together have 42 stuffed animals. Judy has 12 fewer animals than Ramey. How many stuffed animals does each girl have?
Judy = 15
Ramey = 27

Lynn's Reading Chart
Monday	36 pages
Tuesday	42 pages
Wednesday	39 pages
Thursday	0 pages
How could you estimate the total number of pages Lynn read?
○ 42 + 4   ● 40 × 3
○ 42 − 39   ○ 20 × 4

In a deck of 52 cards, there are 2 jokers and 4 each of the number cards, 1–10. The probability of picking a joker is 2 out of 52 or 2/52. Write, as a fraction, the probability of drawing a number 7 card. **4/52**

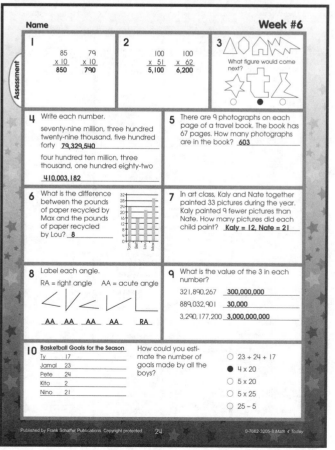

Name — Week # 6

Assessment

1
85 × 10 = 850   79 × 10 = 790
84 × 10 = 840   33 × 10 = 330

2
100 × 51 = 5,100   100 × 62 = 6,200

3 What figure would come next?

4 Write each number.
seventy-nine million, three hundred twenty-nine thousand, five hundred forty **79,329,540**
four hundred ten million, three thousand, one hundred eighty-two **410,003,182**

5 There are 9 photographs on each page of a travel book. The book has 67 pages. How many photographs are in the book? **603**

6 What is the difference between the pounds of paper recycled by Max and the pounds of paper recycled by Lou? **8**
(bar graph: Tom, Beth, Lou, Max)

7 In art class, Kaly and Nate together painted 33 pictures during the year. Kaly painted 9 fewer pictures than Nate. How many pictures did each child paint? **Kaly = 12, Nate = 21**

8 Label each angle.
RA = right angle   AA = acute angle
AA   AA   AA   AA   RA

9 What is the value of the 3 in each number?
321,890,267 **300,000,000**
889,032,901 **30,000**
3,290,177,200 **3,000,000,000**

10 Basketball Goals for the Season
Ty	17
Jamal	23
Pete	24
Kito	2
Nino	21

How could you estimate the number of goals made by all the boys?
○ 23 + 24 + 17
● 4 × 20
○ 5 × 20
○ 5 × 25
○ 25 − 5

Answer Key

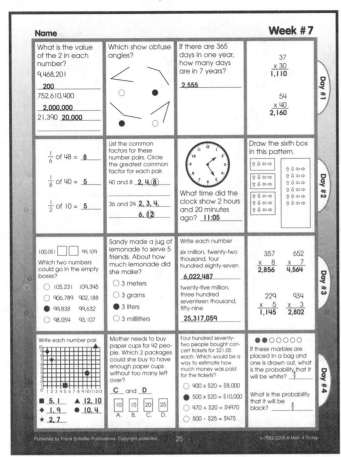

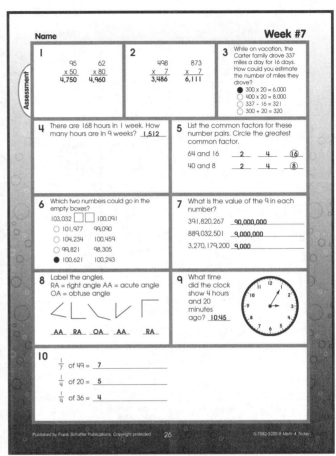

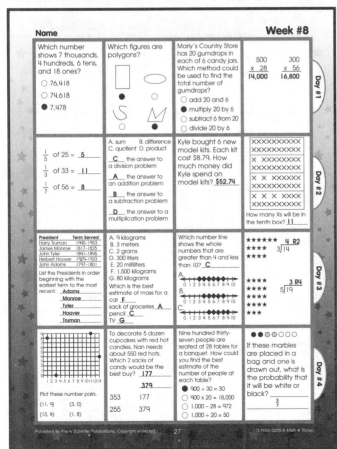

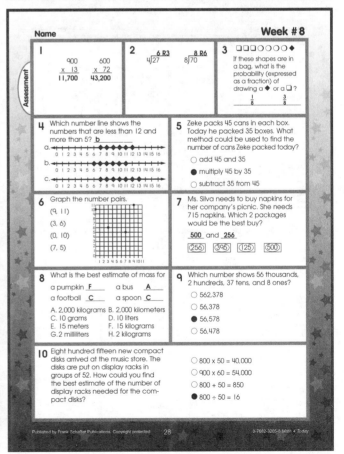

Answer Key

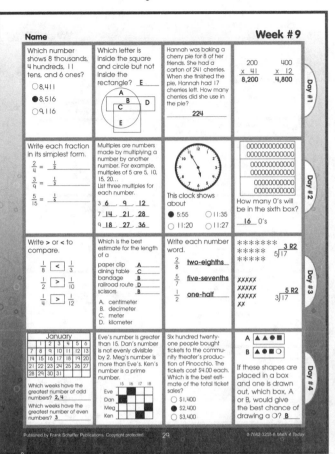

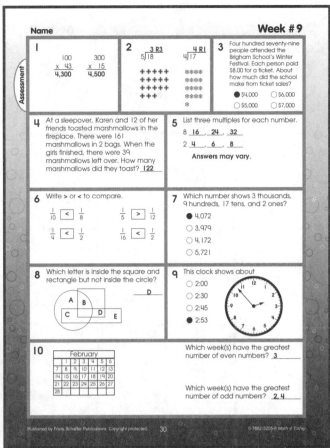

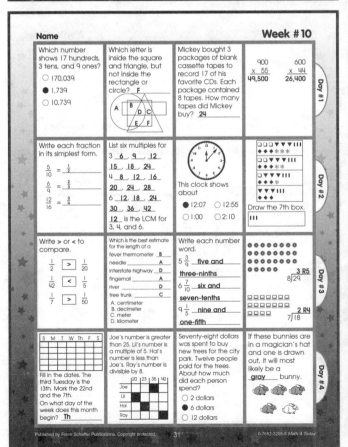

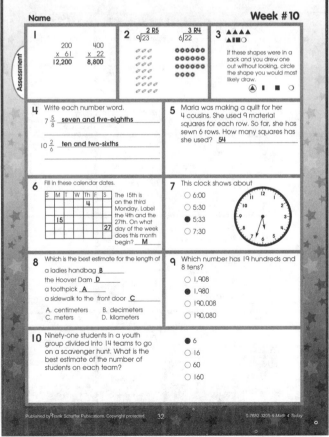

Answer Key

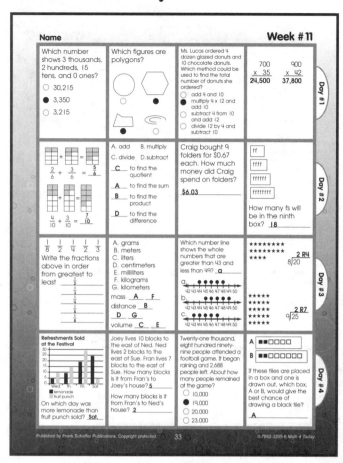

Name — **Week # 11**

Day #1
Which number shows 3 thousands, 2 hundreds, 15 tens, and 0 ones?
○ 30,215
● 3,350
○ 3,215

Which figures are polygons?

Ms. Lucas ordered 4 dozen glazed donuts and 10 chocolate donuts. Which method could be used to find the total number of donuts she ordered?
○ add 4 and 10
● multiply 4 x 12 and add 10
○ subtract 4 from 10 and add 12
○ divide 12 by 4 and subtract 10

700	900
x 35	x 42
24,500	37,800

Day #2
$\frac{2}{6} + \frac{3}{6} = \frac{5}{6}$

$\frac{4}{10} + \frac{3}{10} = \frac{7}{10}$

A. add B. multiply
C. divide D. subtract
C to find the quotient
A to find the sum
B to find the product
D to find the difference

Craig bought 9 folders for $0.67 each. How much money did Craig spend on folders?
$6.03

ff
ffff
ffffff
ffffffff
How many fs will be in the ninth box? **18**

Day #3
$\frac{1}{8}$ $\frac{1}{2}$ $\frac{1}{4}$ $\frac{1}{2}$ $\frac{1}{3}$
Write the fractions above in order from least
$\frac{1}{2}$
$\frac{1}{2}$
$\frac{1}{4}$
$\frac{1}{3}$
$\frac{1}{8}$

A. grams
B. meters
C. liters
D. centimeters
E. milliliters
F. kilograms
G. kilometers
mass **A F**
distance **B**
D G
volume **C E**

Which number line shows the whole numbers that are greater than 43 and less than 49? **a**
a.
42 43 44 45 46 47 48 49 50
b.
42 43 44 45 46 47 48 49 50
c.
42 43 44 45 46 47 48 49 50

****
****
****
$8\overline{)20}$ **2 R4**

*****
*****
*****
*****
*****
$9\overline{)25}$ **2 R7**

Day #4
Refreshments Sold at the Festival
(bar graph: lemonade, fruit punch; Wed, Th, Fri, Sat)
On which day was more lemonade than fruit punch sold? **Sat.**

Joey lives 10 blocks to the east of Ned. Ned lives 2 blocks to the east of Sue. Fran lives 7 blocks to the east of Sue. How many blocks is it from Fran's to Joey's house? **5**
How many blocks is it from Fran's to Ned's house? **2**

Twenty-one thousand, eight hundred ninety-nine people attended a football game. It began raining and 2,688 people left. About how many people remained at the game?
○ 10,000
● 19,000
○ 20,000
○ 23,000

A ■■□□□□
B ■■□□□□□□
If these tiles are placed in a box and one is drawn out, which box, A or B, would give the best chance of drawing a black tile?
A

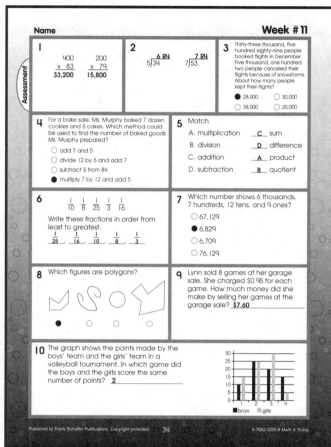

Name — **Week # 11**

Assessment

1
400	200
x 83	x 79
33,200	15,800

2
$5\overline{)34}$ **6 R4**
$7\overline{)53}$ **7 R4**

3 Thirty-three thousand, five hundred eighty-nine people booked flights in December. Five thousand, one hundred two people canceled their flights because of snowstorms. About how many people kept their flights?
● 28,000 ○ 30,000
○ 38,000 ○ 20,000

4 For a bake sale, Ms. Murphy baked 7 dozen cookies and 5 cakes. Which method could be used to find the number of baked goods Ms. Murphy prepared?
○ add 7 and 5
○ divide 12 by 5 and add 7
○ subtract 5 from 84
● multiply 7 by 12 and add 5

5 Match.
A. multiplication **C** sum
B. division **D** difference
C. addition **A** product
D. subtraction **B** quotient

6
$\frac{1}{10}$ $\frac{1}{8}$ $\frac{1}{25}$ $\frac{1}{3}$ $\frac{1}{16}$
Write these fractions in order from least to greatest.
$\frac{1}{25}$ $\frac{1}{16}$ $\frac{1}{10}$ $\frac{1}{8}$ $\frac{1}{3}$

7 Which number shows 6 thousands, 7 hundreds, 12 tens, and 9 ones?
○ 67,129
● 6,829
○ 6,709
○ 76,129

8 Which figures are polygons?

9 Lynn sold 8 games at her garage sale. She charged $0.95 for each game. How much money did she make by selling her games at the garage sale? **$7.60**

10 The graph shows the points made by the boys' team and the girls' team in a volleyball tournament. In which game did the boys and the girls score the same number of points? **2**
(bar graph: boys, girls)

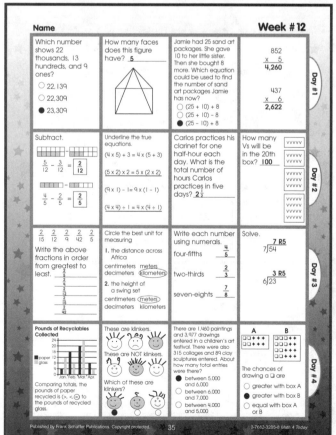

Name — **Week # 12**

Day #1
Which number shows 22 thousands, 13 hundreds, and 9 ones?
○ 22,139
○ 22,309
● 23,309

How many faces does this figure have? **5**

Jamie had 25 sand art packages. She gave 10 to her little sister. Then she bought 8 more. Which equation could be used to find the number of sand art packages Jamie has now?
○ (25 + 10) + 8
○ (25 + 10) - 8
● (25 - 10) + 8

| 852 |
| x 5 |
| 4,260 |

| 437 |
| x 6 |
| 2,622 |

Day #2
Subtract.
$\frac{5}{12} - \frac{3}{12} = \frac{2}{12}$
$\frac{4}{5} - \frac{2}{5} = \frac{2}{5}$

Underline the true equations.
(4 x 5) + 3 = 4 x (5 + 3)
(5 x 2) x 2 = 5 x (2 x 2)
(9 x 1) - 1 = 9 x (1 - 1)
(4 x 4) ÷ 1 = 4 x (4 ÷ 1)

Carlos practices his clarinet for one half-hour each day. What is the total number of hours Carlos practices in five days? **2$\frac{1}{2}$**

How many Vs will be in the 20th box? **100**
vvvvv
vvvvv
vvvvv
vvvvv
vvvvv
vvvvv
vvvvv
vvvvv

Day #3
$\frac{2}{15}$ $\frac{2}{12}$ $\frac{2}{9}$ $\frac{2}{42}$ $\frac{2}{5}$
Write the above fractions in order from greatest to least.
$\frac{2}{5}$
$\frac{2}{9}$
$\frac{2}{12}$
$\frac{2}{15}$
$\frac{2}{42}$

Circle the best unit for measuring
1. the distance across Africa
centimeters meters
decimeters **kilometers**
2. the height of a swing set
centimeters **meters**
decimeters kilometers

Write each number using numerals.
four-fifths $\frac{4}{5}$
two-thirds $\frac{2}{3}$
seven-eights $\frac{7}{8}$

Solve.
$7\overline{)54}$ **7 R5**
$6\overline{)23}$ **3 R5**

Day #4
Pounds of Recyclables Collected
(bar graph: paper, glass; Jan, Feb, Mar, Apr)
Comparing totals, the pounds of paper recycled is (>, <, =) to the pounds of recycled glass.

These are klinkers.
These are NOT klinkers.
Which of these are klinkers?

There are 1,460 paintings and 3,977 drawings entered in a children's art festival. There were also 315 collages and 89 clay sculptures entered. About how many total entries were there?
● between 5,000 and 6,000
○ between 6,000 and 7,000
○ between 4,000 and 5,000

A B
The chances of drawing a □ are
○ greater with box A
● greater with box B
○ equal with box A or B

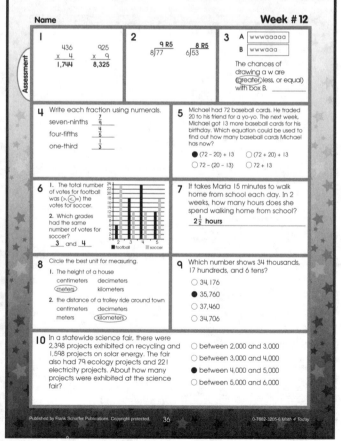

Name — **Week # 12**

Assessment

1
436	925
x 4	x 9
1,744	8,325

2
$8\overline{)77}$ **9 R5**
$6\overline{)53}$ **8 R5**

3 A wwwaaaa
B wwwaaa
The chances of drawing a w are (**greater**, less, or equal) with box B.

4 Write each fraction using numerals.
seven-ninths $\frac{7}{9}$
four-fifths $\frac{4}{5}$
one-third $\frac{1}{3}$

5 Michael had 72 baseball cards. He traded 20 to his friend for a yo-yo. The next week, Michael got 13 more baseball cards for his birthday. Which equation could be used to find out how many baseball cards Michael has now?
● (72 - 20) + 13 ○ (72 + 20) + 13
○ 72 - (20 - 13) ○ 72 + 13

6
1. The total number of votes for football was (>, **<**, =) the votes for soccer.
2. Which grades had the same number of votes for soccer? **3** and **4**
(bar graph: football, soccer)

7 It takes Maria 15 minutes to walk home from school each day. In 2 weeks, how many hours does she spend walking home from school?
2$\frac{1}{2}$ hours

8 Circle the best unit for measuring.
1. The height of a house
centimeters decimeters
meters kilometers
2. the distance of a trolley ride around town
centimeters decimeters
meters **kilometers**

9 Which number shows 34 thousands, 17 hundreds, and 6 tens?
○ 34,176
● 35,760
○ 37,460
○ 34,706

10 In a statewide science fair, there were 2,398 projects exhibited on recycling and 1,598 projects on solar energy. The fair also had 79 ecology projects and 221 electricity projects. About how many projects were exhibited at the science fair?
○ between 2,000 and 3,000
○ between 3,000 and 4,000
● between 4,000 and 5,000
○ between 5,000 and 6,000

Answer Key

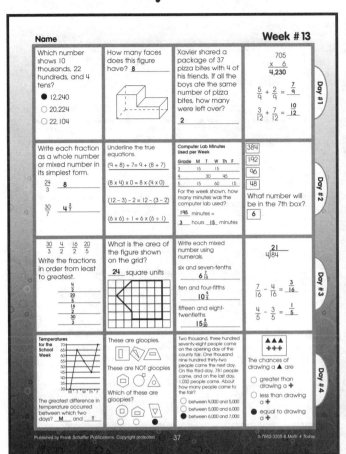

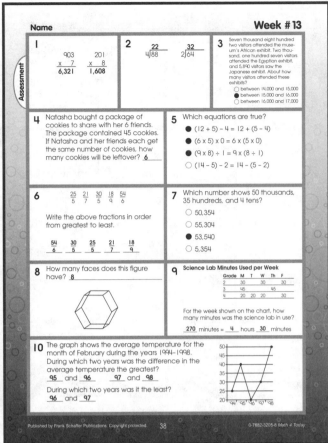

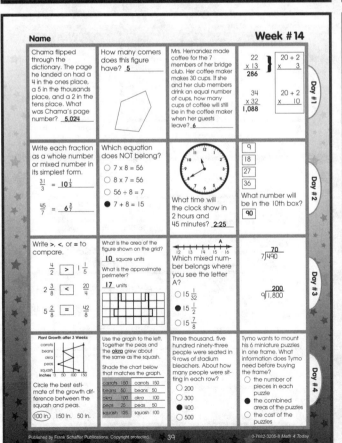

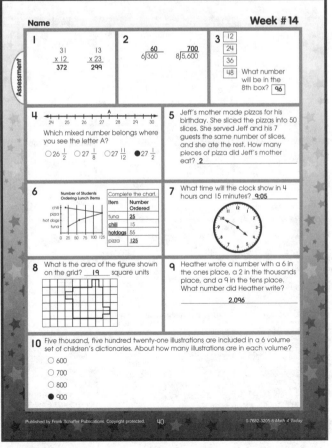

Answer Key

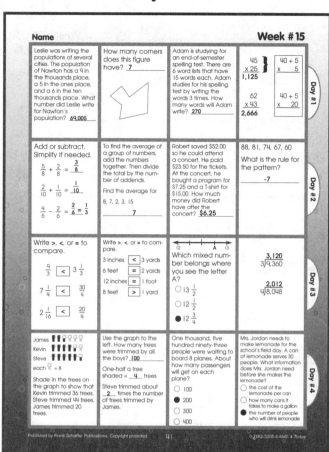

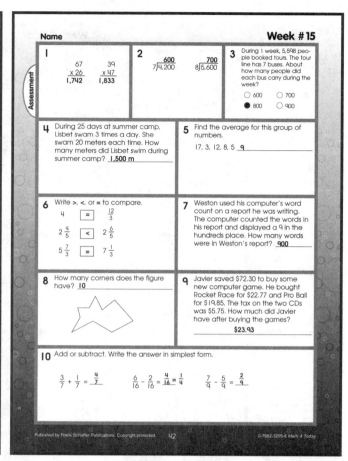

Week #16 (page 43)

Day #1

30,000 + 7,000 + 200 + 3 =
○ 37,230
○ 372,003
○ 30,702,003
● 37,203

Write C if the figures are congruent. Write S if they are similar.
_C_
_C_
_S_

Neva bought 3 packages of gum. Each package has 12 pieces. How can Neva share the gum with 8 of her friends so that she and her friends each get the same number of pieces?
$36 \div 8 = 4\frac{1}{2}$

$\begin{array}{r} 15 \\ \times 75 \\ \hline 1,125 \end{array}$

$\begin{array}{r} 6,247 \\ + 4,788 \\ \hline 11,035 \end{array}$

Day #2

Add or subtract. Simplify.

$\frac{5}{12} + \frac{4}{12} = \frac{9}{12} = \frac{3}{4}$

$\frac{8}{13} - \frac{5}{13} = \frac{3}{13}$

$\frac{12}{32} + \frac{12}{32} = \frac{24}{32} = \frac{3}{4}$

The range of a group of numbers is the difference between the least and the greatest number in the group. The median of a group of numbers is the middle number when the group is arranged from least to greatest.
8, 5, 3, 20, and 2
the range = _18_
the median = _5_

Janette bought nail polish for $3.89, 2 tubes of lip gloss for $2.49 each, and perfume for $4.22. The total after tax was added was $19.54. How much tax did Janette pay on the items she bought?
$1.45

2, 9, 23, 51, 107
What is the rule for the pattern?
+7, +14, +28
+56...

Day #3

Some of the Largest Earth-Filled Dams Measured in Cubic Yards

Tarbela	186,000,000
Oahe	92,000,000
Cornelia	274,026,000
Pati	261,590
Atatürk	110,522

List the names of the dams in order of size from least to greatest. _Atatürk_
Pati _Oahe_
Tarbela _Cornelia_

Write >, <, or = to compare.
24 inches _<_ 3 feet
9 feet _=_ 3 yards
36 inches _=_ 1 yard
10 feet _>_ 2 yards

Which number is read two hundred seventy-five million, nine hundred thousand, forty-six?
● 275,900,046
○ 275,946
○ 200,759,460

$\begin{array}{r} 905 \\ 5\overline{)4,525} \end{array}$

$\begin{array}{r} 805 \\ 9\overline{)7,245} \end{array}$

Day #4

Margie's Gift Wrapping
Sept. ■■■■■
Oct. ■■■■
Nov. ■■■■■■■■■
Dec. ■■■■■■■■■■
each ■ = 50 gifts wrapped
How many gifts were wrapped in October? _150_
How many gifts were wrapped in September? _225_

Use the graph to the left. How many gifts were wrapped during all four months? _1,125_
How many more gifts were wrapped in November and December than were wrapped in September? _525_
How many more ■ would be needed to show 250 gifts wrapped in October? _2_

What is 675,789 rounded to the nearest thousand?
○ 700,000
● 676,000
○ 680,000
○ 674,000

Shane spent $25.00 on vacation souvenirs. His mother spent $40.00, and his dad spent $30.00. Judy, Shane's sister, spent more than Shane and Dad but less than Mother. Which could be true?
○ Judy spent $45.00.
● Judy spent $32.00.
○ Judy spent $29.00.

Week #16 (page 44) — Assessment

1
$\begin{array}{r} 69 \\ \times 47 \\ \hline 3,243 \end{array}$
$\begin{array}{r} 3,987 \\ + 4,776 \\ \hline 8,763 \end{array}$

2
$\begin{array}{r} 906 \\ 4\overline{)3,624} \end{array}$
$\begin{array}{r} 504 \\ 3\overline{)1,512} \end{array}$

3 6, 21, 66, 201
What is the rule for the above pattern?
_×3 +3_

4 Match.
1. three hundred ninety-five million, two hundred six thousand, four hundred one _A_
2. three million, ninety-five thousand, two hundred sixty-one _C_
3. thirty-nine thousand, two hundred sixty-four _B_
A. 395,206,401   B. 39,264   C. 3,095,261

5 Ron bought 3 boxes of juice drinks for his track team. Each box contains 6 drinks. If Ron and his 8 team members each have the same number of juice drinks, how many will each person receive? _2_

6 Operator Assisted Phone Calls from Hotel Farrington
May ☎☎☎☎
June ☎☎☎☎☎
July ☎☎☎☎☎
Aug. ☎☎☎☎☎☎
How many calls were made in June? _440_
How many calls were made in August? _560_
How many more calls were made in August than in May? _240_
In all, how many calls were made? _2,080_

7 Emil earned $57.00 doing odd jobs. Mark earned more than Emil, but less than Jake. Jake earned $72.00. Which could be true?
○ Mark earned $55.00.
○ Mark earned $75.00.
● Mark earned $67.00.

8 Write >, <, or = to compare.
36 inches _>_ 2 feet
3 yards _=_ 9 feet
24 inches _>_ 1 foot
1 yard _>_ 24 inches

9 60,000 + 3,000 + 500 + 4 = _63,504_
500,000 + 80,000 + 2,000 + 1 = _582,001_
20,000 + 300 + 90 + 7 = _20,397_

10 What is 782,432 rounded to the nearest thousand?
○ 780,000
○ 790,000
○ 781,400
● 782,000

What is 816,120 rounded to the nearest thousand?
○ 810,000
● 816,000
○ 822,400
○ 825,000

Answer Key

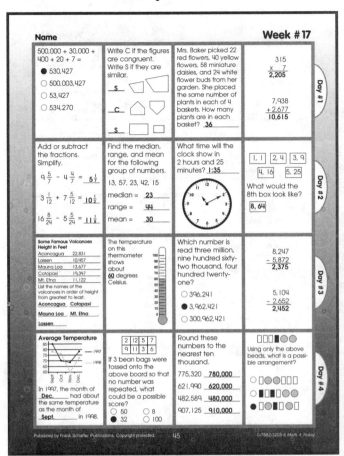

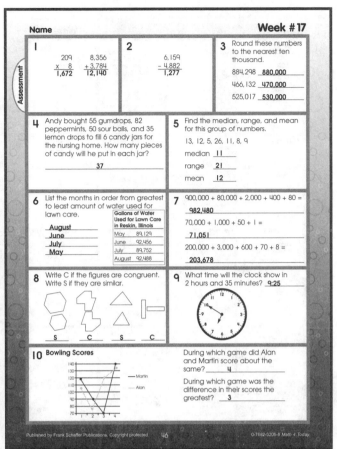

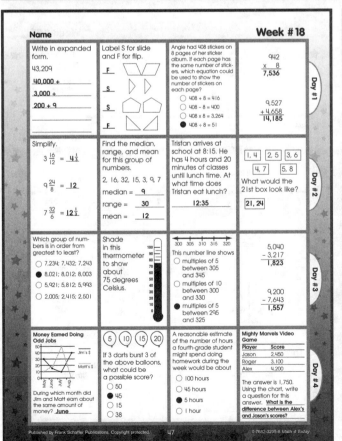

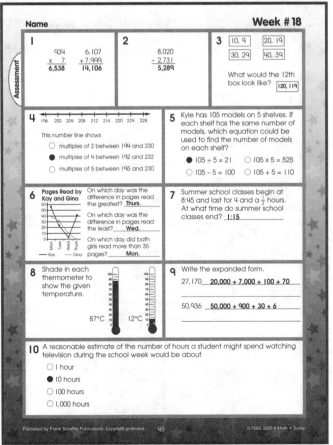

Answer Key

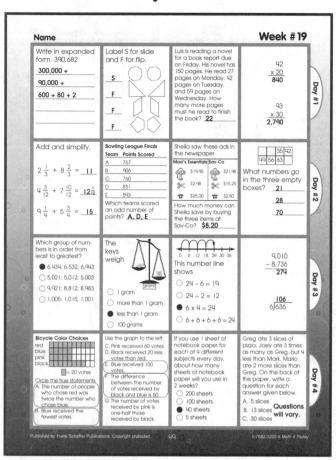

Name — Week #19

Day #1
- Write in expanded form. 390,682
  300,000 +
  90,000 +
  600 + 80 + 2
- Label S for slide and F for flip. S, F, F, F
- Luis is reading a novel for a book report due Friday. His novel has 150 pages. He read 27 pages on Monday, 42 pages on Tuesday, and 59 pages on Wednesday. How many more pages must he read to finish the book? **22**
- 42 × 20 = **840**; 93 × 30 = **2,790**

Day #2
- Add and simplify.
  $2\frac{1}{3} + 8\frac{2}{3} =$ **11**
  $4\frac{3}{12} + 7\frac{10}{12} =$ **12 1/12**
  $9\frac{1}{4} + 5\frac{3}{4} =$ **15**
- Bowling League Finals. Team / Points Scored: A 767, B 906, C 760, D 851, E 593. Which teams scored an odd number of points? **A, D, E**
- Sheila saw these ads in the newspaper. Maxi's Essentials / Sav-Co. How much money can Sheila save by buying the three items at Sav-Co? **$8.20**
- 35 42 / 49 56 63. What numbers go in the three empty boxes? **21, 28, 70**

Day #3
- Which group of numbers is in order from least to greatest? ● 6,434; 6,532; 6,943
- The keys weigh: ● less than 1 gram
- This number line shows: ● 6 × 4 = 24
- 9,010 − 8,736 = **274**; **106** 6)636

Day #4
- Bicycle Color Choices (= 20 votes). Circle the true statements. **A. The number of people who chose red was twice the number who chose blue.**
- Use the graph to the left. E. Blue received 100 votes.
- If you use 1 sheet of notebook paper for each of 4 different subjects every day, about how many sheets of notebook paper will you use in 2 weeks? ● 40 sheets
- Greg ate 3 slices of pizza. Joey ate 3 times as many as Greg... **Questions will vary.**

Published by Frank Schaffer Publications. Copyright protected. 49 — 0-7682-3205-8 Math 4 Today

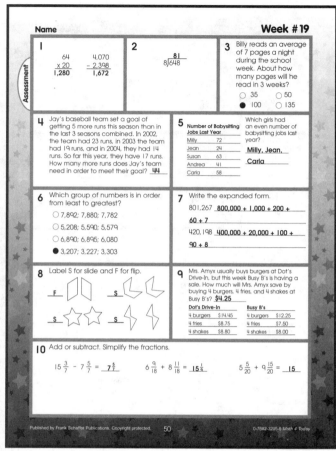

Name — Week #19 (Assessment)

1. 64 × 20 = **1,280**; 4,070 − 2,398 = **1,672**
2. 8)648 = **81**
3. Billy reads an average of 7 pages a night during the school week. About how many pages will he read in 3 weeks? ○ 35 ○ 50 ● 100 ○ 135
4. Jay's baseball team set a goal of getting 5 more runs this season than in the last 3 seasons combined. In 2002, the team had 23 runs, in 2003 the team had 19 runs, and in 2004, they had 14 runs. So far this year, they have 17 runs. How many more runs does Jay's team need in order to meet their goal? **44**
5. Number of Babysitting Jobs Last Year: Milly 72, Jean 24, Susan 63, Andrea 41, Carla 58. Which girls had an even number of babysitting jobs last year? **Milly, Jean, Carla**
6. Which group of numbers is in order from least to greatest? ● 3,207; 3,227; 3,303
7. Write the expanded form. 801,267 **800,000 + 1,000 + 200 + 60 + 7**; 420,198 **400,000 + 20,000 + 100 + 90 + 8**
8. Label S for slide and F for flip. F, S, S, S
9. Mrs. Amyx usually buys burgers at Dot's Drive-In, but this week Busy B's is having a sale. How much will Mrs. Amyx save by buying 4 burgers, 4 fries, and 4 shakes at Busy B's? **$4.25**
   Dot's Drive-In: 4 burgers $14.45, 4 fries $8.75, 4 shakes $8.80
   Busy B's: 4 burgers $12.25, 4 fries $7.50, 4 shakes $8.00
10. Add or subtract. Simplify the fractions.
    $15\frac{3}{7} - 7\frac{5}{7} =$ **7 5/7**; $6\frac{9}{18} + 8\frac{11}{18} =$ **15 1/9**; $5\frac{5}{20} + 9\frac{15}{20} =$ **15**

Published by Frank Schaffer Publications. Copyright protected. 50 — 0-7682-3205-8 Math 4 Today

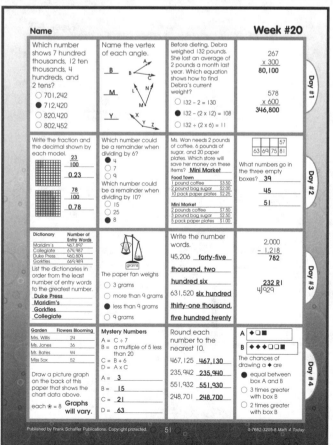

Name — Week #20

Day #1
- Which number shows 7 hundred thousands, 12 ten thousands, 4 hundreds, and 2 tens? ○ 701,242 ● 712,420 ○ 820,420 ○ 802,452
- Name the vertex of each angle. B, M, Y
- Before dieting, Debra weighed 132 pounds. She lost an average of 2 pounds a month last year. Which equation shows how to find Debra's current weight? ● 132 − (2 × 12) = 108
- 267 × 300 = **80,100**; 578 × 600 = **346,800**

Day #2
- Write the fraction and the decimal shown by each model. 23/100, 0.23; 78/100, 0.78
- Which number could be a remainder when dividing by 6? ● 4. Which number could be a remainder when dividing by 10? ● 8
- Ms. Wan needs 2 pounds of coffee, 6 pounds of sugar, and 20 paper plates. Which store will save her money on these items? **Mini Market**
  Food Town: 1 pound coffee $3.50, 2 pound bag sugar $2.00, 10 pack paper plates $2.25
  Mini Market: 2 pounds coffee $7.50, 3 pound bag sugar $2.50, 5 pack paper plates $1.00
- 57 / 63 69 75 81. What numbers go in the three empty boxes? **39, 45, 51**

Day #3
- Dictionary / Number of Entry Words: Maridim's 467,847; Collegiate 674,987; Duke Press 460,809; Gorkties 669,489. List the dictionaries in order from the least number of entry words to the greatest number. **Duke Press, Maridim's, Gorkties, Collegiate**
- The paper fan weighs ● less than 9 grams
- Write the number words. 45,206 **forty-five thousand, two hundred six**; 631,520 **six hundred thirty-one thousand, five hundred twenty**
- 2,000 − 1,218 = **782**; **232 R1** 4)929

Day #4
- Garden / Flowers Blooming: Mrs. Willis 24, Ms. Jones 36, Mr. Bates 44, Miss Sax 52. Draw a picture graph... each ✿ = 8. **Graphs will vary.**
- Mystery Numbers: A = C + 7; B = a multiple of 5 less than 20; C = B + 6; D = A × C. A = **3**, B = **15**, C = **21**, D = **63**
- Round each number to the nearest 10. 467,125 **467,130**; 235,942 **235,940**; 551,932 **551,930**; 248,701 **248,700**
- A ◆□■; B ◆◆◆□■. The chances of a drawing a ◆ are ● equal between box A and B ○ 3 times greater with box B ○ 2 times greater with box B

Published by Frank Schaffer Publications. Copyright protected. 51 — 0-7682-3205-8 Math 4 Today

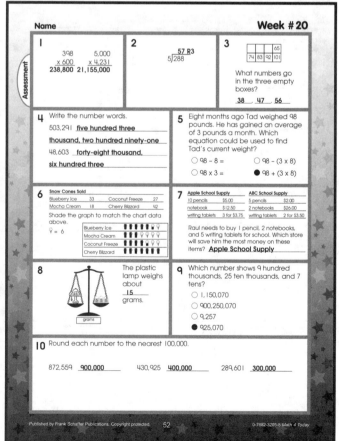

Name — Week #20 (Assessment)

1. 398 × 600 = **238,800**; 5,000 × 4,231 = **21,155,000**
2. 5)288 = **57 R3**
3. 65 / 74 83 92 101. What numbers go in the three empty boxes? **38, 47, 56**
4. Write the number words. 503,291 **five hundred three thousand, two hundred ninety-one**; 48,603 **forty-eight thousand, six hundred three**
5. Eight months ago Tad weighed 98 pounds. He has gained an average of 3 pounds a month. Which equation could be used to find Tad's current weight? ○ 98 − 8 = ○ 98 − (3 × 8) = ○ 98 × 3 = ● 98 + (3 × 8)
6. Snow Cones Sold: Blueberry Ice 33, Coconut Freeze 27, Mocha Cream 18, Cherry Blizzard 42. Shade the graph to match the chart data above. ▽ = 6
7. Apple School Supply: 10 pencils $5.00, notebook $12.50, writing tablets 3 for $3.75. ABC School Supply: 5 pencils $5.00, 2 notebooks $26.00, writing tablets 2 for $3.50. Raul needs to buy 1 pencil, 2 notebooks, and 5 writing tablets for school. Which store will save him the most money on these items? **Apple School Supply**
8. The plastic lamp weighs about **15** grams.
9. Which number shows 9 hundred thousands, 25 ten thousands, and 7 tens? ○ 1,150,070 ○ 900,250,070 ○ 9,257 ● 925,070
10. Round each number to the nearest 100,000. 872,559 **900,000**; 430,925 **400,000**; 289,601 **300,000**

Published by Frank Schaffer Publications. Copyright protected. 52 — 0-7682-3205-8 Math 4 Today

Answer Key

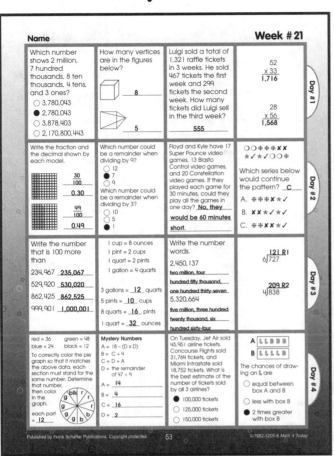

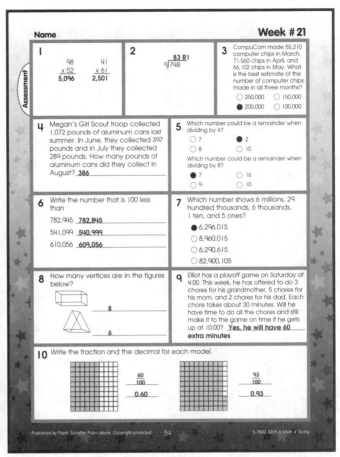

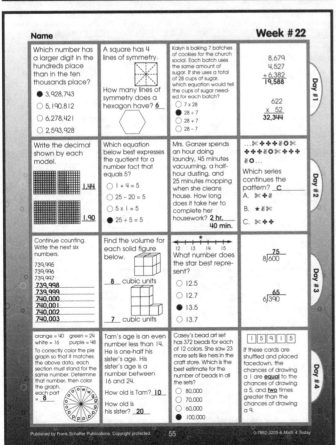

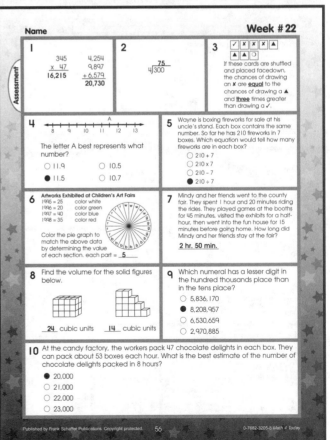

Answer Key

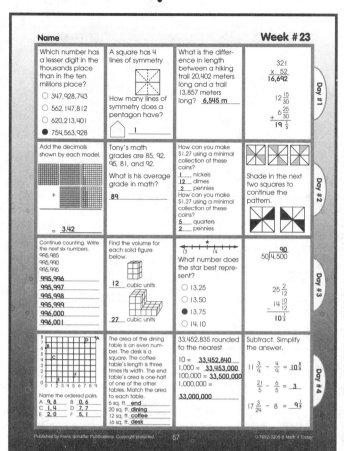

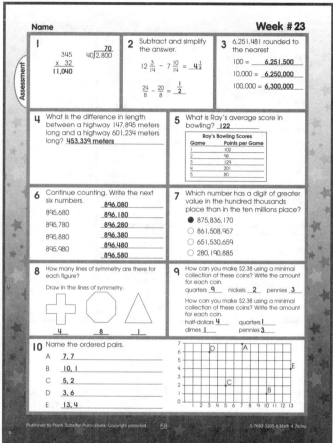

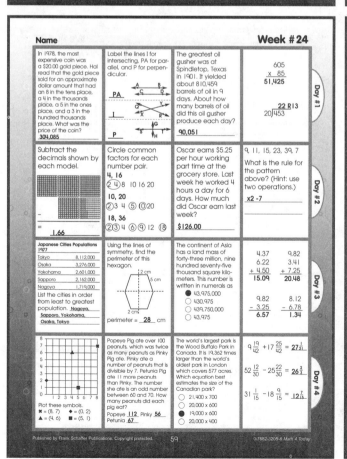

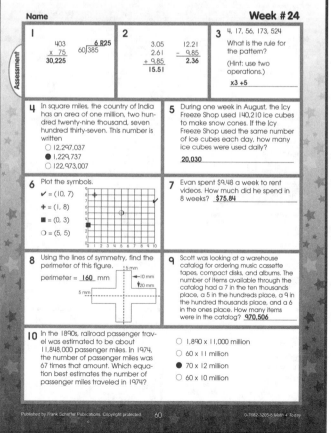

Answer Key

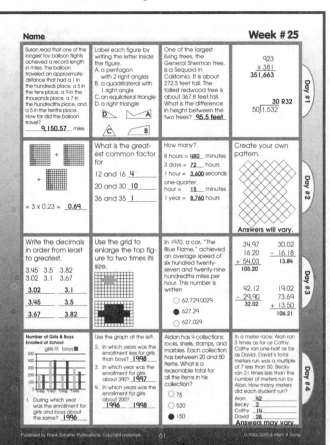

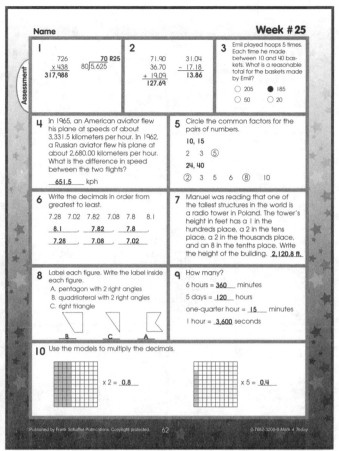

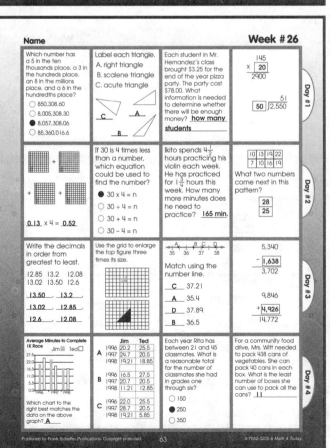

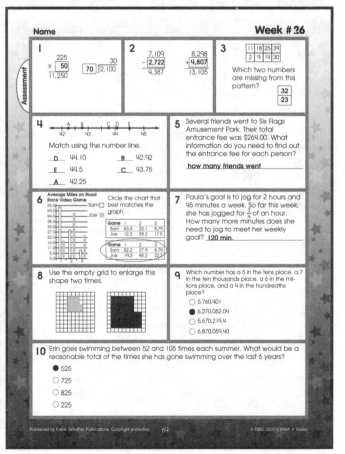

Answer Key

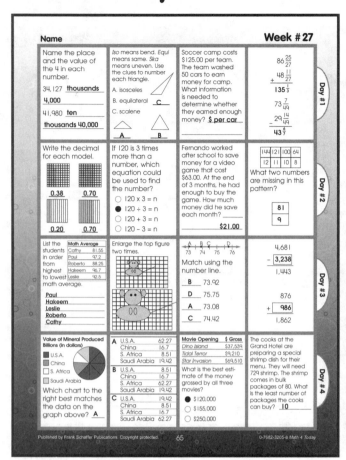

Name — **Week #27**

Day #1

Name the place and the value of the 4 in each number.
34,127 __thousands__
__4,000__
41,980 __ten thousands__ __40,000__

Iso means bend. *Equi* means same. *Ska* means uneven. Use the clues to number each triangle.
A. isosceles
B. equilateral __C__
C. scalene
__A__   __B__

Soccer camp costs $125.00 per team. The team washed 50 cars to earn money for camp. What information is needed to determine whether they earned enough money? **$ per car**

$$86\tfrac{25}{27}$$
$$48\tfrac{11}{27}$$
$$+135\tfrac{1}{3}$$

$$73\tfrac{7}{49}$$
$$29\tfrac{14}{49}$$
$$43\tfrac{6}{7}$$

Day #2

Write the decimal for each model.
__0.38__   __0.70__
__0.20__   __0.70__

If 120 is 3 times more than a number, which equation could be used to find the number?
○ 120 x 3 = n
● 120 ÷ 3 = n
○ 120 + 3 = n
○ 120 – 3 = n

Fernando worked after school to save money for a video game that cost $63.00. At the end of 3 months, he had enough to buy the game. How much money did he save each month? **$21.00**

| 144 | 121 | 100 | 64 |
| 12 | 11 | 10 | 8 |
What two numbers are missing in this pattern?
81
9

Day #3

List the students in order from highest to lowest math average.

Math Average	
Cathy	81.55
Paul	97.2
Roberto	88.25
Hakeem	96.7
Leslie	92.5

__Paul__
__Hakeem__
__Leslie__
__Roberto__
__Cathy__

Enlarge the top figure two times.

Match using the number line.
73 74 75 76
__B__ 73.92
__D__ 75.75
__A__ 73.08
__C__ 74.42

4,681
– 3,238
1,443

876
+ 986
1,862

Day #4

Value of Mineral Produced Billions (in dollars)
■ U.S.A.
■ China
■ S. Africa
■ Saudi Arabia
Which chart to the right best matches the data on the graph above? __A__

A	U.S.A.	62.27
	China	16.7
	S. Africa	8.51
	Saudi Arabia	19.42
B	U.S.A.	8.51
	China	16.7
	S. Africa	62.27
	Saudi Arabia	19.42
C	U.S.A.	19.42
	China	8.51
	S. Africa	16.7
	Saudi Arabia	62.27

Movie Opening	$ Gross
Dino Island	$37,539
Tidal Terror	$9,210
Star Invasion	$69,510

What is the best estimate of the money grossed by all three movies?
● $120,000
○ $155,000
○ $250,000

The cooks at the Grand Hotel are preparing a special shrimp dish for their menu. They will need 729 shrimp. The shrimp comes in bulk packages of 80. What is the least number of packages the cooks can buy? __10__

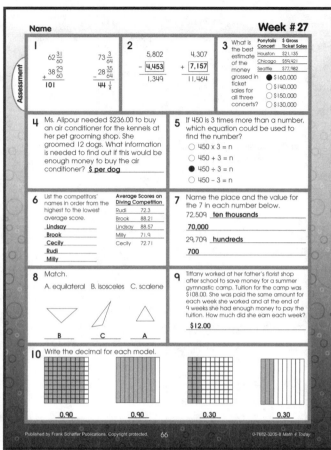

Name — **Week #27**

Assessment

1
$$62\tfrac{31}{60}$$
$$38\tfrac{29}{60}$$
__101__

$$73\tfrac{3}{64}$$
$$28\tfrac{35}{64}$$
__44\tfrac{1}{2}__

2
5,802
– 4,453
1,349

4,307
+ 7,157
11,464

3

Ponytails Concert	$ Gross Ticket Sales
Houston	$21,135
Chicago	$59,421
Seattle	$77,982

What is the best estimate of the money grossed in ticket sales for all three concerts?
● $160,000
○ $140,000
○ $150,000
○ $130,000

4 Ms. Alipour needed $236.00 to buy an air conditioner for the kennels at her pet grooming shop. She groomed 12 dogs. What information is needed to find out if this would be enough money to buy the air conditioner? **$ per dog**

5 If 450 is 3 times more than a number, which equation could be used to find the number?
○ 450 x 3 = n
○ 450 + 3 = n
● 450 ÷ 3 = n
○ 450 – 3 = n

6 List the competitors' names in order from the highest to the lowest average score.

Average Scores on Diving Competition	
Rudi	72.3
Brook	88.21
Lindsay	88.57
Milly	71.9
Cecily	72.71

__Lindsay__
__Brook__
__Cecily__
__Rudi__
__Milly__

7 Name the place and the value for the 7 in each number below.
72,509 __ten thousands__
__70,000__
29,709 __hundreds__
__700__

8 Match.
A. equilateral   B. isosceles   C. scalene
__B__   __C__   __A__

9 Tiffany worked at her father's florist shop after school to save money for a summer gymnastic camp. Tuition for the camp was $108.00. She was paid the same amount for each week she worked and at the end of 9 weeks she had enough money to pay the tuition. How much did she earn each week? **$12.00**

10 Write the decimal for each model.
__0.90__   __0.90__   __0.30__   __0.30__

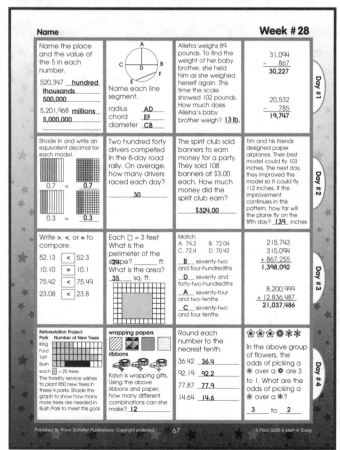

Name — **Week #28**

Day #1

Name the place and the value of the 5 in each number.
520,347 __hundred thousands__ __500,000__
5,201,968 __millions__ __5,000,000__

Name each line segment.
radius __AD__
chord __EF__
diameter __CB__

Alleha weighs 89 pounds. To find the weight of her baby brother, she held him as she weighed herself again. This time the scale showed 102 pounds. How much does Alleha's baby brother weigh? __13 lb.__

31,094
– 867
30,227

20,532
– 785
19,747

Day #2

Shade in and write an equivalent decimal for each model.
0.7 = __0.7__
0.3 = __0.3__

Two hundred forty drivers competed in the 8-day road rally. On average, how many drivers raced each day? __30__

The spirit club sold banners to earn money for a party. They sold 108 banners at $3.00 each. How much money did the spirit club earn? **$324.00**

Tim and his friends designed paper airplanes. Their best model could fly 103 inches. The next day, they improved the model so it could fly 112 inches. If the improvement continues in this pattern, how far will the plane fly on the fifth day? __139__ inches

Day #3

Write >, <, or = to compare.
52.13 __<__ 52.3
10.10 __=__ 10.1
75.42 __<__ 75.49
23.08 __<__ 23.8

Each □ = 3 feet
What is the perimeter of the shape? __24__ ft.
What is the area? __35__ sq. ft.

Match.
A. 74.2   B. 72.04
C. 72.4   D. 70.42
__B__ seventy-two and four-hundredths
__D__ seventy and forty-two-hundredths
__A__ seventy-four and two-tenths
__C__ seventy-two and four-tenths

215,743
315,094
+ 867,255
1,398,092

8,200,999
+ 12,836,487
21,037,486

Day #4

Reforestation Project

Park	Number of New Trees
King	
Ford	
Taft	
Bush	

each ■ = 25 trees
The forestry service wishes to plant 850 new trees in these 4 parks. Shade the graph to show how many more trees are needed in Bush Park to meet this goal.

wrapping papers
ribbons
Kalyn is wrapping gifts. Using the above ribbons and paper, how many different combinations can she make? __12__

Round each number to the nearest tenth.
36.42 __36.4__
92.19 __92.2__
77.87 __77.9__
14.64 __14.6__

In the above group of flowers, the odds of picking a 🌸 over a ❀ are 3 to 1. What are the odds of picking a 🌸 over a ✱?
__3__ to __2__

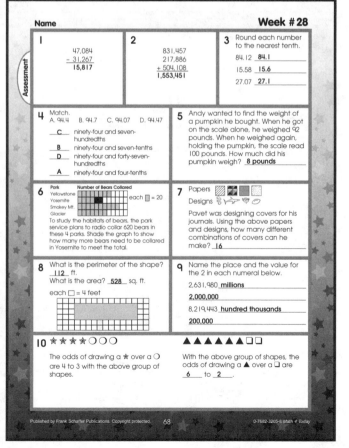

Name — **Week #28**

Assessment

1
47,084
– 31,267
15,817

2
831,457
217,886
+ 504,108
1,553,451

3 Round each number to the nearest tenth.
84.12 __84.1__
15.58 __15.6__
27.07 __27.1__

4 Match.
A. 94.4   B. 94.7   C. 94.07   D. 94.47
__C__ ninety-four and seven-hundredths
__B__ ninety-four and seven-tenths
__D__ ninety-four and forty-seven-hundredths
__A__ ninety-four and four-tenths

5 Andy wanted to find the weight of a pumpkin he bought. When he got on the scale alone, he weighed 92 pounds. When he weighed again, holding the pumpkin, the scale read 100 pounds. How much did his pumpkin weigh? __8 pounds__

6
Park	Number of Bears Collared
Yellowstone	
Yosemite	
Smokey Mt.	
Glacier	

each □ = 20
To study the habitats of bears, the park service plans to radio collar 620 bears in these 4 parks. Shade the graph to show how many more bears need to be collared in Yosemite to meet the total.

7 Papers
Designs
Pavet was designing covers for his journals. Using the above papers and designs, how many different combinations of covers can he make? __16__

8 What is the perimeter of the shape? __112__ ft.
What is the area? __528__ sq. ft.
each □ = 4 feet

9 Name the place and the value for the 2 in each numeral below.
2,631,980 __millions__ __2,000,000__
8,219,443 __hundred thousands__ __200,000__

10 ★★★★○○○
The odds of drawing a ★ over a ○ are 4 to 3 with the above group of shapes.

▲▲▲▲▲▲□□
With the above group of shapes, the odds of drawing a ▲ over a □ are __6__ to __2__.

Answer Key

Week #29

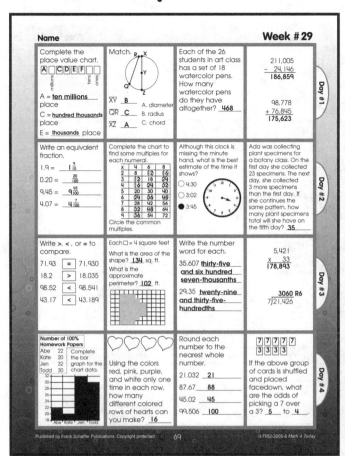

Day #1

Complete the place value chart. A C D E F
A = **ten millions** place
C = **hundred thousands** place
E = **thousands** place

Match. XY **B**; QR **C**; XZ **A**. A. diameter B. radius C. chord

Each of the 26 students in art class has a set of 18 watercolor pens. How many watercolor pens do they have altogether? **468**

211,005 − 24,146 = 186,859
98,778 + 76,845 = 175,623

Day #2

Write an equivalent fraction.
$1.9 = 1\frac{9}{10}$
$0.20 = \frac{20}{100}$
$9.45 = 9\frac{45}{100}$
$4.07 = 4\frac{7}{100}$

Complete the chart to find multiples for each numeral.

x	4	6	8
2	8	12	16
3	12	18	24
4	16	24	32
5	20	30	40
6	24	36	48
7	28	42	56
8	32	48	64
9	36	54	72

Circle the common multiples.

Although this clock is missing the minute hand, what is the best estimate of the time it shows? 4:30 / 3:02 / ● 3:45

Ada was collecting plant specimens for a botany class. On the first day she collected 23 specimens. The next day, she collected 3 more specimens than the first day. If she continues the same pattern, how many plant specimens total will she have on the fifth day? **35**

Day #3

Write >, <, or = to compare.
71.93 **=** 71.930
18.2 **>** 18.035
98.52 **<** 98.541
43.17 **<** 43.189

Each □ = 4 square feet. What is the area of the shape? **134** sq. ft. What is the approximate perimeter? **102** ft.

Write the number word for each.
35.607 **thirty-five and six hundred seven-thousandths**
29.35 **twenty-nine and thirty-five-hundredths**

5,421 × 33 = 178,893
3060 R6 / 7)21,426

Day #4

Number of 100% Homework Papers: Abe 22, Kate 20, Jen 32, Todd 30. Complete the bar graph for the chart data.

Using the colors red, pink, purple, and white only one time in each row, how many different colored rows of hearts can you make? **16**

Round each number to the nearest whole number.
21.032 **21**
87.67 **88**
45.02 **45**
99.506 **100**

7 7 7 7 / 3 3 3 3
If the above group of cards is shuffled and placed facedown, what are the odds of picking a 7 over a 3? **5** to **4**

Week #29 — Assessment

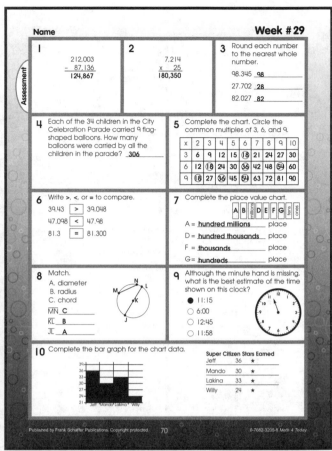

1. 212,003 − 87,136 = 124,867
2. 7,214 × 25 = 180,350
3. Round each number to the nearest whole number. 98.345 **98**; 27.702 **28**; 82.027 **82**
4. Each of the 34 children in the City Celebration Parade carried 9 flag-shaped balloons. How many balloons were carried by all the children in the parade? **306**
5. Complete the chart. Circle the common multiples of 3, 6, and 9.

x	2	3	4	5	6	7	8	9	10
3	6	9	12	15	18	21	24	27	30
6	12	18	24	30	36	42	48	54	60
9	18	27	36	45	54	63	72	81	90

6. Write >, <, or = to compare. 39.43 **>** 39.048; 47.098 **<** 47.98; 81.3 **=** 81.300
7. Complete the place value chart. A B D E F G. A = **hundred millions** place; D = **hundred thousands** place; F = **thousands** place; G = **hundreds** place
8. Match. A. diameter B. radius C. chord. MN **C**; KL **B**; JL **A**
9. Although the minute hand is missing, what is the best estimate of the time shown on this clock? ● 11:15 / 6:00 / 12:45 / 11:58
10. Complete the bar graph for the chart data. Super Citizen Stars Earned: Jeff 36, Mando 30, Lakina 33, Willy 24

Week #30

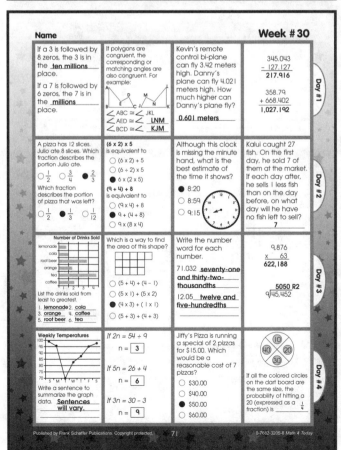

Day #1

If a 3 is followed by 8 zeros, the 3 is in the **ten millions** place.
If a 7 is followed by 6 zeros, the 7 is in the **millions** place.

If polygons are congruent, the corresponding or matching angles are also congruent. For example:
∠ABC ≅ ∠**JKL**
∠AED ≅ ∠**LNM**
∠BCD ≅ ∠**KJM**

Kevin's remote control bi-plane can fly 3.42 meters high. Danny's plane can fly 4.021 meters high. How much higher can Danny's plane fly? **0.601 meters**

345.043 − 127.127 = 217.916
358.79 + 668.402 = 1,027.192

Day #2

A pizza has 12 slices. Julio ate 8 slices. Which fraction describes the portion Julio ate? $\frac{1}{2}$ $\frac{3}{4}$ ● $\frac{2}{3}$
Which fraction describes the portion of pizza that was left? $\frac{1}{2}$ ● $\frac{1}{3}$ $\frac{1}{12}$

(6 × 2) × 5 is equivalent to: (6 × 2) + 5 / (6 + 2) × 5 / ● 6 × (2 × 5)
(9 + 4) + 8 is equivalent to: (9 × 4) + 8 / ● 9 + (4 + 8) / 9 × (8 × 4)

Although this clock is missing the minute hand, what is the best estimate of the time it shows? ● 8:20 / 8:59 / 9:15

Kalui caught 27 fish. On the first day, he sold 7 of them at the market. If each day after, he sells 1 less fish than on the day before, on what day will he have no fish left to sell? **7**

Day #3

Number of Drinks Sold: lemonade, cola, root beer, orange, tea, coffee. List the drinks sold from least to greatest. 1. **lemonade** 2. **cola** 3. **orange** 4. **coffee** 5. **root beer** 6. **tea**

Which is a way to find the area of this shape? (5 + 4) + (4 − 1) / (5 × 1) + (5 × 2) / ● (4 × 3) + (1 × 1) / (5 + 3) + (4 + 3)

Write the number word for each number.
71.032 **seventy-one and thirty-two-thousandths**
12.05 **twelve and five-hundredths**

9,876 × 63 = 622,188
5050 R2 / 9)45,452

Day #4

Weekly Temperatures. Write a sentence to summarize the graph data. **Sentences will vary.**

If 2n = 54 ÷ 9; n = **3**
If 5n = 26 + 4; n = **6**
If 3n = 30 − 3; n = **9**

Jiffy's Pizza is running a special of 2 pizzas for $15.00. Which would be a reasonable cost of 7 pizzas? $30.00 / $40.00 / ● $50.00 / $60.00

Dart board: 10 / 40 / 20 / 30. If all the colored circles on the dart board are the same size, the probability of hitting a 20 (expressed as a fraction) is $\frac{1}{4}$

Week #30 — Assessment

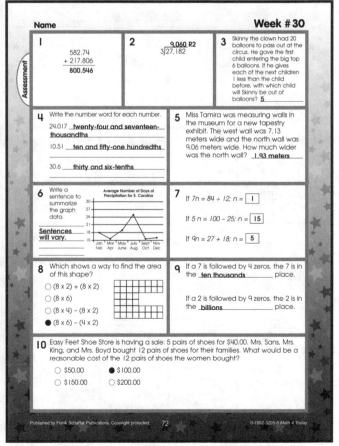

1. 582.74 + 217.806 = 800.546
2. 9,060 R2 / 3)27,182
3. Skinny the clown had 20 balloons to pass out at the circus. He gave the first child entering the big top 6 balloons. If he gives each of the next children 1 less than the child before, with which child will Skinny be out of balloons? **5**
4. Write the number word for each number.
   24.017 **twenty-four and seventeen-thousandths**
   10.51 **ten and fifty-one hundredths**
   30.6 **thirty and six-tenths**
5. Miss Tamira was measuring walls in the museum for a new tapestry exhibit. The west wall was 7.13 meters wide and the north wall was 9.06 meters wide. How much wider was the north wall? **1.93 meters**
6. Write a sentence to summarize the graph data. Average Number of Days of Precipitation for S. Carolina. **Sentences will vary.**
7. If 7n = 84 ÷ 12; n = **1**
   If 5n = 100 − 25; n = **15**
   If 9n = 27 + 18; n = **5**
8. Which shows a way to find the area of this shape? (8 × 2) + (8 × 2) / (8 × 6) / (8 × 4) − (8 × 2) / ● (8 × 6) − (4 × 2)
9. If a 7 is followed by 4 zeros, the 7 is in the **ten thousands** place.
   If a 2 is followed by 9 zeros, the 2 is in the **billions** place.
10. Easy Feet Shoe Store is having a sale: 5 pairs of shoes for $40.00. Mrs. Sans, Mrs. King, and Mrs. Boyd bought 12 pairs of shoes for their families. What would be a reasonable cost of the 12 pairs of shoes the women bought? $50.00 / ● $100.00 / $150.00 / $200.00

Answer Key

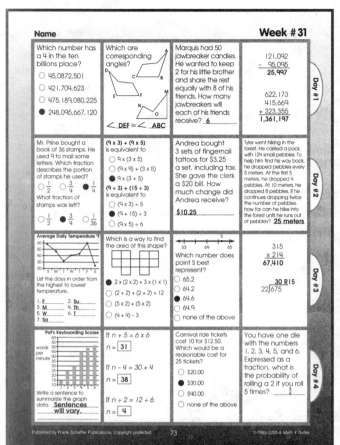

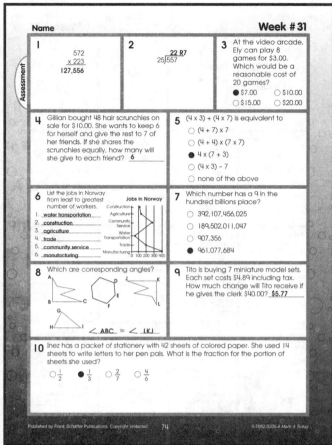

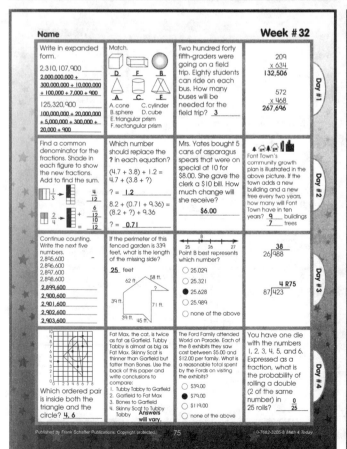

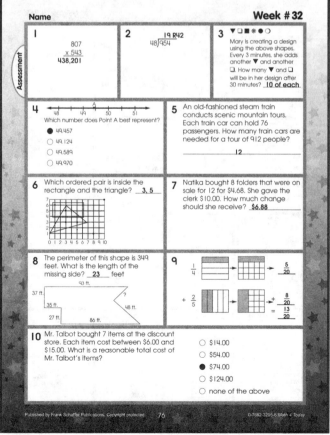

Answer Key

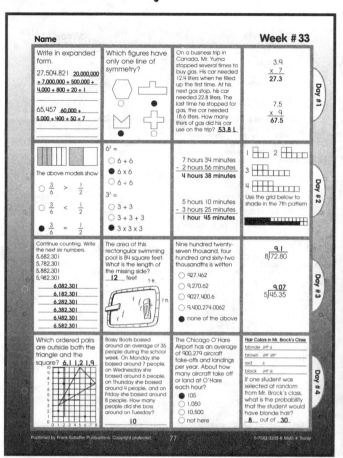

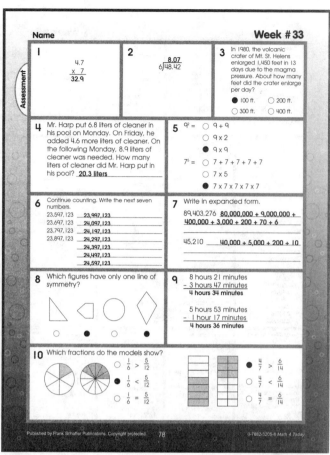

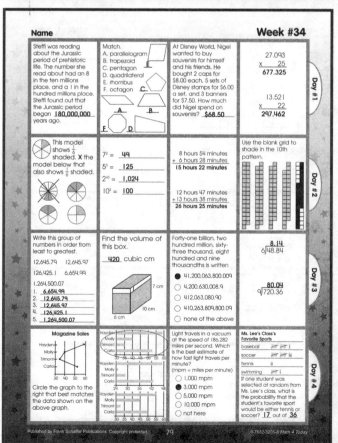

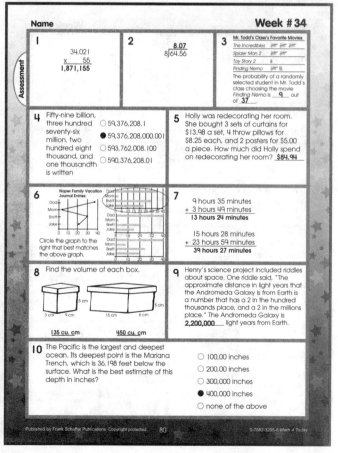

Answer Key

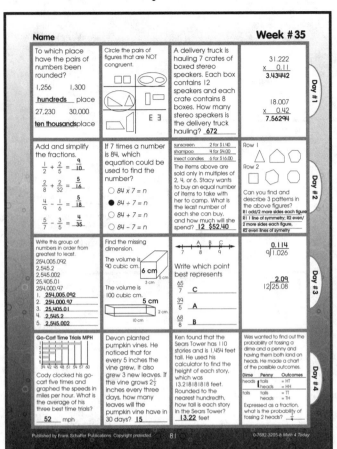

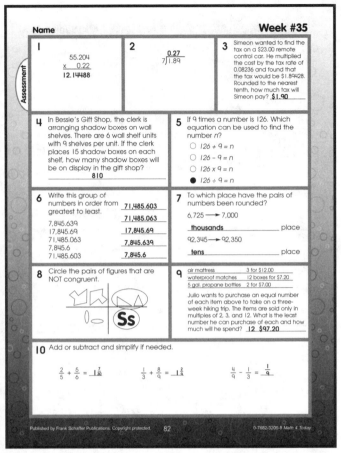

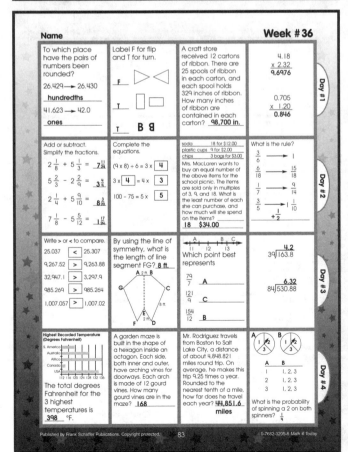

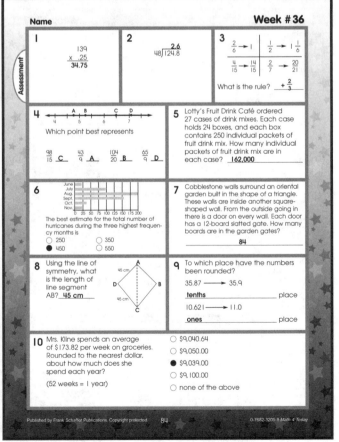

Answer Key

Published by Frank Schaffer Publications. Copyright protected.

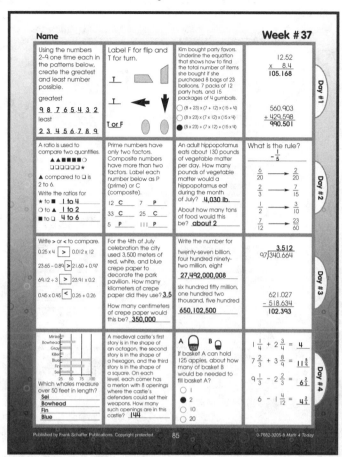

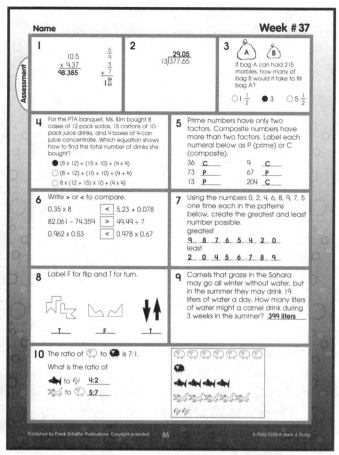

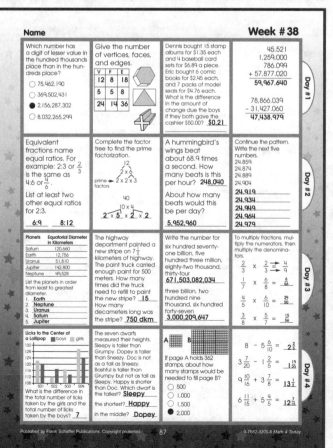

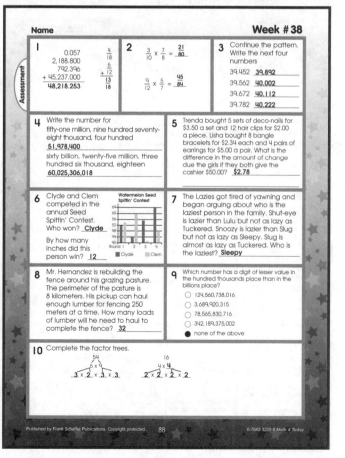

0-7682-3205-8 *Math 4 Today*

Answer Key

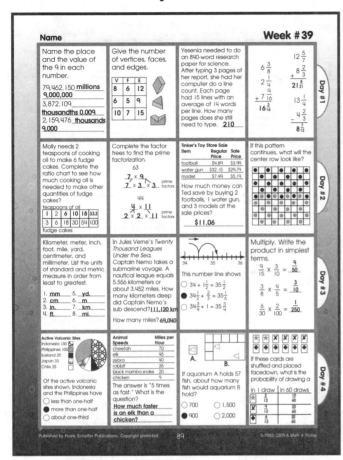

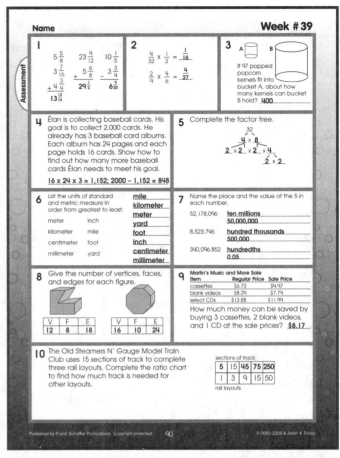

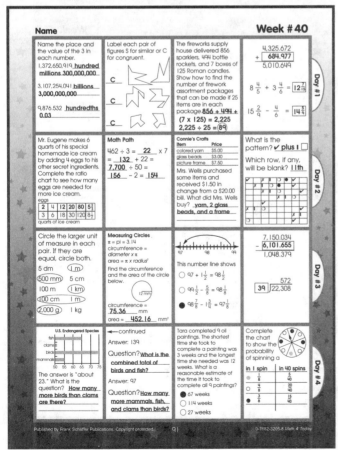

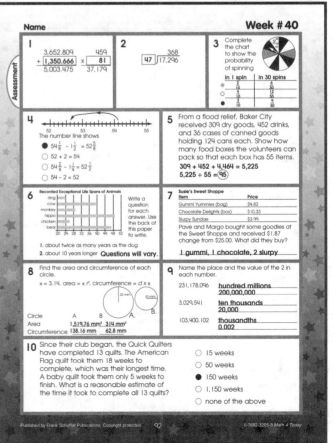

112

0-7682-3205-8 *Math 4 Today*